IRRESISTIBLE

A story of how passionate leadership & smart design
changed a school—and a community.

WORDSWORTH
press

Published by Wordsworth Press
Cincinnati, OH 45202
Copyright © 2017, SHP Leading Design
Manufactured in the United States of America

"The best way to predict the future is to create it."

Peter F. Drucker

We dedicate this book to Ridgemont Local School District. We applaud Emmy Beeson, the former superintendent, for her visionary leadership and her tireless, inspiring commitment to a world-class, future-ready education. And we congratulate the staff, teachers, parents, volunteers and citizens of Ridgemont who took the future in their own hands and, together, created something truly remarkable.

TABLE OF CONTENTS

INTRODUCTION   8

Section I—RIDGEMONT: STEPPING (BOLDLY) INTO THE FUTURE

Chapter 1
OF PLACES & PEOPLE   11

Chapter 2
THE OLD GUARD   15

Chapter 3
A MAN'S WORLD   19

Chapter 4
TO LEARN IS TO SERVE, TO SERVE IS TO LEARN   24

Chapter 5
THE SUPER   30

Chapter 6
THE ELECTIONEER   36

Chapter 7
COMMUNITY REFLECTION   42

Chapter 8
THE TURNING POINT   44

Chapter 9
ENVISIONING RIDGEMONT   48

Chapter 10
CHANGE OF PLANS   56

Chapter 11
BUYING IN   60

Chapter 12
A NEW BEGINNING   66

Chapter 13
THE FUTURE OF RIDGEMONT   78

Section II—THE SIX ATTRIBUTES OF IRRESISTIBLE SCHOOLS

Chapter 14
REIMAGINING THE EDUCATIONAL EXPERIENCE   86

Chapter 15
WHAT IT WILL MEAN TO LEARN IN THE FUTURE   89

Chapter 16
ATTRIBUTE #1: LIFELONG LEARNING   92

Chapter 17
ATTRIBUTE #2: WHOLE-LIFE LEARNING   96

Chapter 18
ATTRIBUTE #3: INDIVIDUALIZED LEARNING   99

Chapter 19
ATTRIBUTE #4: INVOLVED AND BLENDED LEARNING   103

Chapter 20
ATTRIBUTE #5: UNBURDENED COLLABORATION   106

Chapter 21
ATTRIBUTE #6: ADAPTIVE AND DYNAMIC SPACES   108

Conclusion
9 BILLION SCHOOLS   111

INTRODUCTION

Just as the Industrial Revolution dramatically reshaped the American landscape, so too is the Technological Revolution reshaping what it means to learn and work in the United States. Those manufacturing jobs, prized just a couple generations ago, are no longer the norm. Preparing students for work is no longer about achieving a basic level of competence and going off with their lunch pail or on to a university. The world has changed. The economy has changed. The nature of work has changed. So why is it that education has largely remained the same?

We've seen the United States go from a world leader in education to something much less. We've seen other nations rocket toward the top, in terms of achievement in core subjects like math and science. And we've responded by challenging schools to catch up to a new standard. We've removed creativity and learning from education, as a means of focusing on standardized achievement. We've allowed politics and funding mechanisms to place a premium on the percentage of the whole, as opposed to the achievement of the individual.

It's easy to think that this kind of education is a relic of the past, but that's not true. Isn't the controversial No Child Left Behind education bill a call for greater standardization? We have spent 100 or more years believing that education was a thing a person did when they were young, until they were ready to join the work force.

The truth is that education has changed, but the change is often slow and subtle. Currently we are in the midst of a seismic shift in what it means to learn in the 21st century; and SHP Leading Design is on the forefront. For more than 110 years, we have been designing and building spaces to support learning, from one-room schoolhouses to the buildings of today that are preparing the students of tomorrow. But it's not enough to build future-thinking schools.

At its heart, education is about the student, the teacher and the environment in which instruction takes place. Students change. Teachers adapt. And the physical space must keep pace, in order to ensure the appropriate canvas for all types of learning to take place.

While it's always dangerous to paint with too broad a brush, there are a few general characteristics about today's students that pretty much everyone would agree to. They are not just technologically savvy, but technologically dependent. They are unusually collaborative, and very open with their thoughts and experiences. In response, educators talk of the value of critical thinking and digital literacy over the rote memorization of facts. They recognize the importance of encouraging students to link information to experience and action. They agree that students need to be empowered to own their education and given an outlet for creative, collaborative learning.

Armed with this knowledge, educators are adjusting curricula, updating teaching philosophies, and getting parents and students onboard.

While we see these trends and developments across all of our clients, one—Ridgemont Local School District in central Ohio—has an especially interesting, instructive and inspiring story to share. For anyone looking to improve their schools and their community, Ridgemont Local School District offers many lessons. The first half of this book tells that story in detail.

The second half of this book details six key attributes that we believe shape the best in education—and the spaces in which it occurs—in this, our exciting, mind-blowing (if at times frightening) 21st century.

We hope you find this book insightful. More so, we hope it motivates you to imagine and help bring into existence 21st-century-worthy, irresistible education in your community.

Section I

RIDGEMONT:
STEPPING (BOLDLY) INTO THE FUTURE

1

OF PLACES & PEOPLE

A school is more than a building to which we send our children to learn. It's more than a place to host afterschool activities and sports. A school is a reflection of the community it serves—that community's priorities, its beliefs and values. Or, at the very least, it should be.

Our job is to explore, to question, to ask what makes a community a community, to ascertain what that community believes and needs, and to bring to life latent aspirations in the form of a building. In most cases, we discover what is already there. We listen to the voices of the schools, of the local businesses, of community leaders, of students and find the "through lines," or "organizing principles," that will empower our designs. Schools, while functionally similar, are unique and distinct. They are the settings for our formation as students, as professionals, as educators, as people.

Most communities know what they stand for, what they believe, even if it goes unexpressed. Our job is to crystalize it and express it in design. But every once in a while, we are faced with an opportunity to help a community come together for the first time (or perhaps in a long time), to change course, to express a new set of values and core beliefs. This was the case with Ridgemont. Walking through that school is like experiencing a community as it redefines itself and its future. To know the story of how that school came to be is to witness the possibility of change and the risk that goes with it. But in order to understand the power of Ridgemont, you need a little history and context.

Chances are good you've never heard of Ridgeway, Ohio. There's not a lot of reason why you should have. It's a small town. There is a main street, but not the kind you're probably imagining. No Norman Rockwell storefronts. No charming central square. Just a gas station and convenience store nestled close to the railroad tracks, where in one transaction you can fill up your car, pick up a case of soda, a carton of milk, some eggs and a thick breakfast sandwich hearty enough to carry you through lunch and beyond.

It's the kind of place where they recognize you as an outsider and have a theory about why you might be there. Step out of that convenience store, breakfast sandwich in hand, with a tie on your neck or heels on your shoes, and someone might ask if you work for the Honda plant down the road. Or maybe Monsanto—they have a presence nearby too.

The town is a collection of small, humble houses occupied by proud local people along shady, quiet streets. It's the kind of place in which you could imagine people leaving their doors unlocked, though they probably don't. Not a lot of sidewalks, but not a lot of need for them either. You see bikes leaned against trees in yards, comfortable-looking chairs on covered porches, next to large picture windows with no shades drawn.

Google Maps will tell you that Ridgeway is a little more than an hour to the west and north of Columbus—Ohio's largest, fastest-growing city and capital. In the city, life moves fast. But in Ridgeway, life moves a bit more slowly, a bit more cautiously. Talk to residents, and you get the sense that progress has its time and place; but more than anything, connection and consistency are cherished above experimentation and anything—culturally anyway—perceived as cutting-edge.

In that regard, Ridgeway is like any other small town in America. Driving through corn and soybean fields, endless expanses of rolling, productive landscape dotted by the occasional factory, processing plant, rural airport or high school football stadium, you don't see Ridgeway coming. It's just a cluster of trees on the horizon.

If you find yourself in a place like Ridgeway, you might not notice. Or maybe you do, and your mind wonders: What do people do around here? How slow and easy life must be. You start to apply expectations to the world that you are in. You expect things about the people. You expect things about social lives. You expect certain things about the kids in the schools. You may or may not expect the people to be rallying around a school system that is standing tall and redefining what education can and should be. You may not expect a teacher to change her students' lives by pushing them to do bigger, better work. You may not expect a lifelong resident, alumnus of the district, veteran teacher and retiree to be leading the charge for change. You may not expect a superintendent to be laying everything on the line to take a gamble on a new kind of education, a way of teaching kids to be not only proficient students, but fully developed humans active in leading their communities and prepared to take on the world. You wouldn't expect, in this tiny little town, a revolution in the way Americans educate their young.

And yet that's exactly what is happening in Ridgeway. It's not just a tiny town like so many other small towns spread across the great expanses of the American exterior. It is neither sleepy, nor simple. It is neither stuck in its ways, nor passively standing by as the world leaves it in its rearview mirror. Ridgeway is home to audacious people unafraid to dream big, not intimidated by their hometown's tiny size.

This is the story of how a small town rises up in the face of expectation—or a lack thereof—to design its own destiny. It is the story of some dedicated, passionate and visionary leaders—not politicians or CEOs—who brought a town together to form a common vision for an undefined future. It is the story of a century-old architecture and design firm willing to throw tradition and expectation to the wind and help rewrite the rules of education. It is a story that might make you think differently about the little towns that you find yourself passing through. This is the story of how a small town in the Midwest is leading a new way of thinking about America's future.

And it all begins with the schools.

2

THE OLD GUARD

One of the challenges of working on a school project, particularly in a small community, is legacy. In places in which families establish roots, generations walk the same halls and memory is indelible, designers often have to account for old wounds, old politics and old scripts that set in like indigo and are difficult to wash off. It's impossible to talk about the schools that serve Ridgeway and Mount Victory, Ohio, without talking about the merger. If you are from the area, you remember the controversy that led to excitement when, back in 1963, Ridgeway Schools were combined with their most favorite rivals, Mount Victory, to form Ridgemont Local School District. And, if you are Cheryl France, you remember the excited nerves that preceded the first day at that new combined school.

Cheryl is one of those Ridgeway people: the ones who know everything about every person and place related to Ridgeway; the ones who know the history behind the politics, the people behind the stories—and, yes, the story of the schools.

"I remember that first day of school," she says, recalling day one of her high school junior year. "I remember the principal, Helen Winder, and her secretary, Evelyn Keller, who came from Mount Victory, standing at the front door, welcoming us all in. I had been so nervous. What would it be like? What would happen? But there she was, standing at the front door, telling us everything was going to be great."

Cheryl also remembers wondering what would happen to her school, her friendships in the new combined school. It was all so intimidating and confusing, which might seem strange to an outsider. After all, both districts were small and the communities close enough that it might take all of an hour to meet all of the new kids, to form new friendships, to cocreate a common identity. But change is never easy, especially for students. School is so much a part of a person's identity at young ages, any change feels like a shift in the very fabric of your being.

If you took a stroll down the halls of the school that Cheryl walked into that day a half century ago, you would get the feeling that change is something that has come slowly, if at all, to the students of Ridgemont. After the merger the Mount Victory building housed grades K-8, and Ridgeway School was home to grades 1-4 and 9-12. When Cheryl told this story, Mount Victory held grades K-6, and Ridgeway housed grades 7-12. Cheryl's high school was small, compact and efficient. The hallways were narrow. Above the neatly hung lockers were pictures of the graduating classes going all the way back to that first one. The hairstyles and collar widths showed a progression of fashion, and the march toward better camera technology was revealed in the sharpness of the photos; but the thing that might have struck you was the otherwise complete lack of change. Every year roughly the same number of kids—between 35 and 45—and roughly the same balance of gender. Nearly homogeneous, in terms of race. Nearly identical in poise and composure. In those photos you would see the generational nature of places and schools like this. Parents in some photos, their children further down the hall.

The rooms of the school were square, industrial in their cinder-block construction, made as homey as possible by teachers trying to liven up their classes with colorful charts and posters. It would not be hard to imagine students like Cheryl tucked beneath their desks, as part of the nuclear-readiness drills that defined our reflection of school in the Cold War era.

Cheryl returned to Ridgemont after graduating college. She taught English. She taught music. She convinced students to participate in musicals; and, even now, the memory of some of those shows warms her heart. It's plain, written all over her face when she tells her stories, the pride that she had in her students, in her school, in her town.

But pride will only take you so far. After 36 years in the classroom, Cheryl was ready to retire. She was ready to get out of the school in which she had spent so much of her life. She was ready to settle down. Her granddaughter had moved in with her, and Cheryl was ready to focus on her needs, to make sure she grew up to be the kind of woman who would feel the same kind of pride that Cheryl had. And, after nearly 40 years of constancy, Cheryl realized that the Ridgemont schools weren't really going anywhere.

It's not that Cheryl—animated and bright, the kind of person who can make you feel like the only person in a room—had lost hope. It's just that there is only so much hope a person can have before they need to let go. She had done her time. She had put her heart into Ridgemont Local School District and its students. She had seen students like Apryl Ealy take to her lessons, dive into her studies and graduate, only to come back a few years later and become teachers themselves. Cheryl seems particularly proud of Apryl, who remembers Cheryl's lessons in literature and grammar as being an impetus for her desire to become a teacher.

Apryl graduated from Ridgemont in 1975, and returned after college to join Cheryl as an English teacher, specializing in teaching gifted seventh- through 12th-graders. She spent 23 years in the Ridgemont schools (stretched over a longer period of time, as she stayed home to help raise her own family). And for a long time, she witnessed the steady decline into sameness, the same sort of year-after-year, do-it-because-we-always-have feeling come over the schools and the community at large.

"I saw it happen," says Apryl, whose bright voice and inner confidence shine through when she speaks. "Over time, I just saw apathy about the schools, especially among the young families."

Education was a cost of doing business, and business wasn't good. It was so different from that first day of school back in 1963, when Cheryl was nervous, but excited about the possibilities, about the new challenges and opportunities that the combined district brought. It was the apex of hope, of progress that was followed by a glacial melt downward over the years.

Many people in the area had given up on the schools. We would see that when we began working on the first campaign to get a bond issue passed for the new school. Every community has doubters, people skeptical of schools, people who assume that school leaders have bad intentions. There was some of that here as well; but more than anything, it seemed like a certain kind of contagious apathy had settled into the Ridgemont community. After a half-century of slow atrophy, Ridgemont Local School District and the communities that it served needed more than just hope. It needed a catalyst. It needed a match to ignite change, to push the schools, where no one expected too much, past the verge and onto a different path.

"Everything was status quo for a long time," Cheryl says. "Things just stayed the same. It was fine at first; but if things stay the same for too long, they start to fall apart. It was just status quo until the year before I retired. I always felt like we were on the verge of something great, but just on the verge."

"That's," says Cheryl, "when Stephanie happened."

If things stay the same too long they fall apart.

3

A MAN'S WORLD

When gathering input to influence the design of a school, we listen to a lot of people: community leaders, school leaders, students, industry, etc. Often, among the various voices, a few stand out for their clarity and their strength, for the sense of purpose and vision that they convey. Every project needs these voices. Sometimes they belong to administrators; sometimes they belong to outspoken opponents or passionate parents. It's not always the case, but many times the voices will belong to a teacher or a group of teachers who have strong beliefs about what the school needs, what the current school lacks, what stands in the way of their educating students properly.

But it's rare that a single teacher has such a profound impact on establishing the vision of a school, a district and a community. Stephanie Jolliff is that rare teacher—educator, really—with such conviction and purpose. Her input, her voice was instrumental in helping establish the design principles and functional designs of Ridgemont Local School District. But it almost didn't happen at all.

Stephanie lives in a man's world. Or at least that's what she was told when she interviewed for the position at Ridgemont in 2006. Agriculture education was men's work. Teaching students about crops and equipment was no task for the fairer sex. What kind of woman, after all, would want to do the kind of work that sends you home at night with dirt under your fingernails and grease smeared across your face?

It turns out that Stephanie Jolliff is exactly that kind of woman and always has been. She grew up on a farm in western Ohio, the family business, and enjoyed the kind of work for which she demonstrated an early aptitude and passion. It was honest work, work that relied as much upon the integrity of the farmer as it did the contents of the soil. She knew from an early age that agriculture was in her future and that making that future a reality would mean being willing to stand up straight in the face of a lot of other people telling her that she was a woman in a man's world.

She's just the kind of person who doesn't mind standing up, especially for something that she believes in. She doesn't mind being the outlier. So when the old superintendent of Ridgemont was interviewing her, telling her that she might not want the teaching position in the schools because of her gender, it was just another person to stand up in front of straight and tall. There will always be those people. No use letting this one stop her.

Seeing Stephanie, it's easy to question her position in agriculture. The image of most agriculture teachers is probably not all that different from the one you conjure in your mind when thinking about wood-shop, or welding-shop, teachers—rough, broad, haggard. But she is none of those things. She is tall and stands with the sort of poise and confidence that you might expect from a CEO. Her red-tinted, blonde hair curls over her face, where her smile is soft and warm. She's quiet, almost contemplative when she speaks, not the kind of person whom you might expect to be smashing through gender barriers. Her intelligence is obvious, as is her passion when she tells stories like the one about Corey, a student she taught in her first year at Ridgemont.

Corey showed a lot of promise; but a lot of promise in agriculture at Ridgemont generally didn't amount to much. Over the years it had been consistent that a quarter of a graduating class would go to college—mostly girls—some would go into the military, and half would go into the family farm or a related business right out of school. Maybe some secondary technical education, but usually straight to the fields, the garages and the processing plants so common to the area. Agriculture was a subject that you took in high school, but it was not necessarily a subject that you studied in the pursuit of something. Today Corey serves on the Ridgemont Local School District Board of Education and encourages visionary programs, like the programming that he was brave enough to be part of when Stephanie came to Ridgemont.

Corey was different. In him, Stephanie, who was breaking rules and expectations just for having the job, saw more than just promise; she saw passion. That year, 2007, she encouraged Corey, just as she did most other students; but Corey had a sincere passion for agriculture. Stephanie supported his agricultural interests, and he took to being pushed. It fueled him. And the more passionate he became about agriculture—not just as something most of the kids from his class would end up in, but as something he could excel at—the more opportunities Stephanie sought for his advancement. Corey excelled at state and national Future Farmers of America (FFA) events, which amplified Stephanie's expectations.

As students entered the agricultural education program over the next few years, they engaged in meaningful service-learning projects that focused on local and global issues. Stephanie was always looking for ways to network her students with global leaders who would serve as mentors, to prepare them to be innovators. Another student who led the program into pivotal experience was Cody Seiler. Cody was a freshman who was not sure that he wanted to take on leadership roles right away; but Stephanie saw great potential in his ability. Eventually she begged, borrowed, cajoled and convinced others to help; and that year Cody designed a project featured in the World Food Prize competition in Iowa.

The World Food Prize is a program that bills itself as "the foremost international award recognizing—without regard to race, religion, nationality or political beliefs—the achievements of individuals who have advanced human development by improving the quality, quantity or availability of food in the world," on its website: www.worldfoodprize.org. It is basically part Model UN and part TED conference on the topic of food. It's a place in which the best and brightest students in the world of agriculture come to share their solutions to some of the planet's most daunting challenges about feeding an economically diverse and constantly growing population.

It goes without saying that students from Ridgemont had never really taken part in the World Food Prize, much less excelled at it. But that was before Stephanie, before Cody, before a student with promise met a teacher who cared more about defining the future than about adhering to the past. Cody did well in the competition. People from much larger districts noted how well prepared and poised he was. They noted the quality of his project, his innovative thinking.

"We were so proud of him," says Apryl Ealy, who joined Stephanie and Cody at the conference, thanks in large part to the generosity of a supporter who paid for her airfare personally. "He stood up there and made us so proud."

Apryl and Stephanie found in each other the confidence to push for greatness, the comfort to break down walls and challenge the established culture in the Ridgemont schools. In very little time, Stephanie would breathe new life and excellence into an agriculture program that had withered from the status quo. She reinvigorated FFA, which had always been an important part of Ridgemont, by pushing students farther and farther, by combining innovation and technology with a demand for excellence. And tiny Ridgemont, a school system that no one expected much from, went from the status quo to state and even national championship titles.

Scroll down the timeline on the Ridgemont FFA Facebook page, and the news is flooded with championships and awards—something that Stephanie Jolliff is too humble to talk about, but which amazes Cheryl France to this day.

"Imagine it, Ridgemont as national champions," she says with the enthusiasm that can only come from a deep and profound pride. "Who would think tiny little Ridgemont would be the champions of anything, let alone winning national championships again and again? And it's all because of Stephanie."

Indeed, it's the right combination of passion, ability and a blindness to limitations that has driven Stephanie and her core belief that nothing is impossible; it has only yet to be achieved.

Of course, not everyone in Ridgemont was as quick to adulation as Cheryl France. There have been other teachers who thought Stephanie was going too far—community members who, despite demonstrable success, were skeptical of the woman stirring up such a commotion in a man's world. But if there was a specific moment to be pointed to, a tipping point when the status quo of Ridgemont was shaken, it was that moment in 2006, when Stephanie Jolliff took the job teaching agriculture knowing there would be skeptics; knowing there would be those who would believe she was going too far; knowing some people would see her as just a woman in man's world. Because it was in that moment that a spark was lit that would lead to a whole different kind of fire that would end up with learning becoming not just something students were expected to do, but something irresistible to kids like Cody and everyone who would come after.

4

TO LEARN IS TO SERVE, TO SERVE IS TO LEARN

Agriculture was central to the community priorities and needs for Ridgemont Local School District. Early in our work, understanding how this kind of career technical education could serve as a centralizing factor in the design of the new school became apparent. Cody's project sparked a new sense of educational possibility in Ridgemont, a new way of thinking about how students learn and how that learning can be translated from rote memorization to real-world application.

While this was happening in Ridgemont classrooms, attempts to pass a bond issue to upgrade and update facilities were failing. Ridgemont first tried to pass a bond issue for a new K-6 school and renovations to the 7-12 building in 2007. That failed bond attempt led to another try in the spring of 2008, which also failed, and yet another in the fall of 2008, which was removed from the ballot by the Board of Education prior to the vote, due to lack of community support.

The contrast between the energy in Stephanie's classroom and the community's apparent appetite for improved schools was striking. Somehow Ridgemont would have to help community members understand the dire situation that their school buildings were in and what kind of learning could happen in upgraded facilities.

No small challenge.

Over the years SHP Leading Design has seen a lot of changes in education. We've incorporated new technologies, new approaches and new priorities into our designs. With Ridgemont project-based learning was beginning to take root. The notion of students using practical application of knowledge in order to bolster education was beginning to gain momentum. In the spring of 2010, the district applied for a state grant to explore how project-based learning might be applied to the district's curriculum, to expand on the momentum that Stephanie Jolliff had created.

Ellen Erlanger and Kathy Meyer, of the Columbus-based non-profit consulting firm Partnerships Make a Difference, were hired with that grant money, to conduct a series of seminars and professional-development sessions to help Ridgemont's staff understand the potential for project-based and service learning in the schools.

"Project-based learning is about creating authentic experiences in education," says Kathy. "It's designed to create connections for students between the lessons they are learning and real-world applications."

Instead of learning skills in a vacuum, this type of learning is designed around an end use, with real-world significance. Math lessons, once taught through formulas and memorization, become tools to accomplish a desired outcome. Technology lessons, once relegated to the computer lab, become integrated into projects designed to encourage problem-solving. English goes from the rules of grammar to the art of persuasive communication. History transforms from lessons in dusty classrooms and textbooks to interactions between students and older citizens in the community who can lend context and perspective to the facts in the books.

Traditional classroom work is delayed gratification, Kathy and Ellen believe. It involves keeping students and learning compartmentalized in classrooms and out of the world, with the promise of one day becoming useful.

"Project-based learning is an effort to stop viewing education as delayed gratification," Kathy says. "The traditional way of educating is forcing students to learn a bunch of facts and figures, lessons and content that they will be able to use when they become a 'real person' some day."

Traditional education is static and passive. Project-based and service learning are active and hands-on. They support the notion that students can have an impact at any age. This concept is nothing new. Back when she was an undergrad and grad student at the University of Michigan, Ellen says that her professors were extolling the value of making learning practical, of creating connections between learning and knowledge, knowledge and application, application and impact.

But when she began her career, she quickly understood the disconnect between the things that she learned in college and the way the world works. Despite the theories and approaches that educators were learning in college, school systems didn't work in a way to support the necessary continuing education and extra planning that teachers need in order to make project-based learning work.

"I had an opportunity early in my career in the classroom to incorporate some of the authentic learning principles that I studied in college," she says. "I was an eighth-grade American-history teacher and created a project to team students up with older members of the community, to learn about events that they lived through. I saw firsthand the impact on the students."

She saw how it changed and deepened the students' experiences and understanding of the lesson content. To be able to make a connection, to be able to contextualize something being learned in school with the real-life experiences related to it changes education. That connection is the difference between knowing something and understanding it.

Ellen continued to pursue opportunities for her students to engage in project-based learning throughout her career in the classroom and as an administrator in the Upper Arlington school district, where she expanded the approach to teachers across the district. It was in her administrative role that she connected with Kathy, who was in a similar role in the nearby Worthington school district. Together they explored ways to bring project-based learning into their and neighboring districts and, eventually, at the state level.

"We both spent 40 years working in education," Kathy says. "When we retired, we thought we would do some consulting on the side, part time. We didn't expect it to become what it is today—a full-time job."

Indeed, project-based learning has taken off in recent years, mostly as a response to standardized testing, Kathy says.

"For a long time, people in education have suppressed a desire to incorporate project-based learning into curriculum, because all of the focus has been on standardized-test scores," says Kathy. "But that suppression led to repression, which we're now seeing has led to a kind of rebellion."

Teachers don't want to teach static information, Kathy and Ellen argue. They don't want their efforts and instruction to be boiled down to memorization without retention. They want to help students learn and understand, apply and incorporate lessons into life; and they understand and have seen the evidence—like the work that Stephanie Jolliff has done—of the benefits of project-based learning in student achievement.

All that has been missing is the district resolve to help teachers bring these methods into the classroom, through training and support.

Training and support were exactly why Kathy and Ellen first were introduced to Ridgemont in 2010. The workshops that they ran with teachers were designed to inform and encourage staff about project-based learning approaches. One stood out to Ridgemont's staff among the possible ways of leading project-based learning in schools: service learning.

If project-based learning is about tying concept to application, service learning takes that approach one step farther, by tying the lessons taught in school to solving specific challenges facing a community.

"You've probably heard about robot-building competitions that are held in schools around the country," says Kathy. "That's project-based learning. It's tying what the kids are doing in school to a specific task: building a robot.

"Service learning would take that one step farther," she continues. "The service-learning approach would be to reach out to people in the community with disabilities that prevent them from performing certain tasks and then building a robot designed to complete that specific task."

Service learning ties concept to application and adds an element of intention that Kathy and Ellen say engages students not only academically and intellectually, but emotionally. Students shift from being captive participants in a static educational experience to proactive solvers of community problems. This extra vector captivates students, regardless of past academic performance, and engages students in a much deeper way.

They cite an example of a project completed by eighth-grade students at Buckeye Middle School near Columbus as emblematic of the value of service learning. Students there tackled the issue of traumatic brain injury as a leading cause of death in children and youth, particularly injuries suffered as part of athletic competition. The students there dove into the problem; but rather than simply learning about brain injury and how trauma impacts kids, they studied the issue and worked with nearby universities to develop a Concussion Management Plan for the Columbus City School Board.

When a teacher is focused solely on preparing students for a standardized test, that teacher might never consider taking on such a demanding project. But what makes it even more impressive is the fact that the students who led the project were, prior to their involvement, classified as underachievers.

"The difference is astounding," Kathy says. "Just think if those same kids had been taught that way through their entire education. They probably would never have been underachieving. In fact, I'd bet that they would be considered high-level readers by the time they got to eighth grade."

Service learning was appealing to many members of the staff

at Ridgemont, and some of the principles were applied immediately after the 2010 instruction from Kathy and Ellen. First-grade students were given the challenge of solving a community problem. They chose the problem of providing presents for children stuck in the hospital.

The first-graders analyzed the problem and decided to buy toys for hospitalized youth. But first they had to devise a way to buy presents, raise money, activate the community around the project and track results. They designed a project to make Christmas gift tags from old Christmas cards. They asked local businesses to sell them to raise the funds for the gifts, which meant applying their math skills to set goals, their language skills to communicate with business owners, their fine-motor skills to make the gift tags, and organizational skills to plan and execute the whole thing.

Students were enthusiastic about the project. They latched on to it. Associating the goal of community good with lessons in school captivated students, and teachers reported increased engagement in the classroom.

Service learning gained a foothold in Ridgemont schools; but in order for the spark to ignite a flame, someone at the district level would need to usher in a systemic change.

Someone like Emmy Beeson.

5

THE SUPER

Designing and building a new school is a partnership. As the designers, we are trusted to guide school leaders and administrators, the community and stakeholders through a tested process to plan against not only the needs of today, but also those of the future. Schools are built not just to meet today's standards, but to be the foundation of a vision. SHP has always been a proactive partner in designing that vision, and there are literally dozens of factors that go into that design.

Ridgemont Local School District was not like other districts that we've worked with. Unlike suburban districts, which experienced population booms in growing economies, or urban districts that have been desperately trying to hold on to precious resources, Ridgemont's population had remained largely unchanged for decades. Resources were scarce, as you might expect; and the vision for education, though it had been energized a bit in recent years, thanks to the incorporation of service and project-based learning, was still relatively flat. The need for a new school was driven largely by deterioration of the old schools. We worked closely with the community and stakeholders to understand priorities, but establishing a true vision for the future couldn't be accomplished by us alone.

We needed a partner with as much energy and enthusiasm

for the project as we had. For Ridgemont to become what it did, the community needed an advocate—someone who was unafraid of tackling the status quo and unashamed to demand more. It could not be a design firm alone that would lead them there.

They got that person in the form of a new superintendent, Emmy Beeson.

She walks quickly. It's not the kind of walk that suggests she's in a hurry, though it would be understandable if she were. She has that kind of schedule, the kind that keeps her going from predawn to the late evening. But it's not the walk of someone in a rush or someone who is late. Rather, it's the walk of a person who knows where she is going.

On paper Emmy is an unlikely visionary. We tend to think that those come from places like Silicon Valley or Menlo Park. In education it's assumed that you pay your dues, put in your time playing by the rules before you start to nudge them, prod them around the edges. But that's not the way Emmy operates.

She began her career like many administrators, as a teacher. "I was in the classroom for six years," she said. "I taught, well, everything." Social studies in fifth through eighth grade, physical education for kids in elementary and junior high schools, keyboarding, reading, history. She was one of those teachers who cared more about teaching than what she taught. But in everything—every subject, every class—she had her eyes on the main office. She wanted to be a principal, to have that kind of influence over how a school is run.

"When you're a teacher, you look around and you always think, 'I can do that better.'" She smiles at the thought. You get the sense that, for Emmy, there is always better. "When I was growing up, I was going to be the first female President of the United States. I wanted to help humanity. Then I wanted to be a high school teacher."

Again she smiles. Again, a small acknowledgment of the conflict that she feels about her own ambition. She's a woman of faith, a humble woman who just can't help herself. She can't help that desire to do more—not have more (it isn't about greed), but to push herself and have a greater impact. Being a principal, she reasoned when she was a teacher, was her ultimate calling. She could have an impact and facilitate better ways of doing things for her school, her community and her students—always the students.

Ultimately the principal's job was not to be. Instead, her path took her from the classroom to the central office. She became the curriculum director of a district not unlike Ridgemont to the east. It was a bigger district, but still rural, still a vital part of the community. Emmy admits that she didn't know what she was getting into when she took the job, only that it meant hard work and opportunities to make things better. But not knowing how to do something has never stopped Emmy from doing that something with excellence.

And so, in the days of No Child Left Behind and standardized testing, when educating a community's young people became highly politicized and a lightning-rod subject around breakfast tables and coffee tables throughout the country, Emmy took on the task of designing and improving the teaching curriculum of an entire district.

Balancing state and federal mandates with local realities and needs and then translating all of that into a plan that will drive education forward is no small task. But spend more than five minutes with Emmy, and you'll realize that there has not yet been a task developed that she can't complete. For a lot of people in education, curriculum director is the kind of position that might be a late-career goal. Teacher, department head, vice principal, principal. Maybe a shot at the central office before you begin to think about retirement.

As of 2015, there were 611 school districts in Ohio and one that bleeds over into Indiana. This means that there are 611 top jobs in districts, which sounds like a lot; but the trend is shrinking. A century ago there were more than 2,600 districts in the state. Budget cuts, urban and suburban growth, and consolidation from shrinking populations mean that districts continue to merge and shift and bend.

Her experience as a curriculum director told Emmy that she might have a better way of getting things done. Or, more accurately, that there was a better way, and she wanted to be the one who

helped to uncover it. So when the job as the Ridgemont superintendent opened up, it got her interested. Sure, she had never been a chief
executive of a district; but a lack of experience had never stopped her
before.

It helped that Ridgemont was a small district, the kind where
teachers right out of college spend a year or two to build their resume,
before heading for the bigger districts for better pay and more access
to resources. And the same went for administrators. It was a good
place to get your feet wet and move on. The only people who stayed
were the people who had never left in the first place—the people and
teachers who grew up there, had roots there, had never entertained
the idea of leaving.

But Emmy doesn't look at the world as a series of stepping
stones. Her ambitions are not based upon personal achievement. They
are based on an innate desire to make an impact. And, in Ridgemont,
she saw the opportunity to do just that. She also saw an enormous
challenge to be tackled. It was a perfect opportunity for her.

"I suppose a lot of what's happened since then comes from
my not knowing any better," Emmy says. She smiles, tickled by her
own naiveté. "I didn't have a lot of experience coming in. I didn't have
expectations about what you can and can't do; and I think because of
that, I've been able to do what I think is right."

When Emmy came to Ridgemont, the district was in flux.
Stephanie Jolliff and Apryl Ealy were making headway in the community with their leadership in agricultural education and service learning. But the community was torn. Even within the walls of the schools,
there were separate camps—teachers looking forward and innovating,
those who believed the old way of doing things was fine and didn't
need to be changed, and those who only took the job at Ridgemont
to build a resume. The first group captured Emmy's attention. The last
was to be expected. Every year a quarter of the staff at Ridgemont
will turn over—young teachers right out of college getting offers closer to big cities or where they came from, older teachers retiring.

It was the second group that challenged her—the group that

seemed entrenched, the ones that looked to teachers like Stephanie and Apryl with skepticism. The ones who just wanted to show up and do their time. Not necessarily bad teachers. In fact, they were often quite good at their jobs. It was simply that they didn't like change all that much. It was these teachers—and what organization doesn't have employees like these?—whom Emmy needed to understand more, because these teachers seemed to reflect a lot of what was happening in the community at large.

When she came on board, Emmy found herself in the middle of a heated atmosphere around attempts at bond issues that would provide for the construction of a new school for Ridgemont. The old schools were just that—old—and needed a lot of work. For a long time, the district had been solving problems with duct tape and elbow grease, but the time had come when they were just getting too expensive to fix and repair. The buildings were outdated and, some worried, way past their time.

But elections like these in communities as small as Ridgemont are difficult, fragile affairs. For one thing, the economically challenged farm community didn't have a lot of money to throw around. For another, many in the community thought that the schools were good enough for them—and their parents—and so were still good enough for today's youth. Couple those things with a lack of vision for the future that had only grown more myopic as the years had gone by and a change in the leadership, and you had a dicey situation for the new person sitting at the superintendent's desk. Remember that prior to Emmy's taking over, the district had run two bond issues that failed and placed a third bond issue on the ballot that was pulled before voting day, due to lack of community support.

Immediately upon taking the job, Emmy had to begin campaigning for operating money to keep the district afloat. In the four months between being hired and the vote, she had to get to know people, be out in the community, listen and strategize. "I called Cheryl France, because I knew she was against the bond issue. I wasn't sure where she stood on the operating levy, and I knew she had been in the schools for a very long time," Emmy says. She needed a different perspective, and Cheryl had never been afraid to share hers with anyone.

"I went to Emmy's office, and we talked for a long time," says Cheryl. "I was against the bond issue when I sat down; and by the time we were done talking, I had changed my mind. I left with 'Vote Yes' signs under my arm."

Cheryl had not only changed her mind about the ballot issue to fund the new schools; she had changed her mind about the schools themselves. Emmy convinced her to believe in the future of Ridgemont and, in turn, in Emmy herself. A school-board position was opening up, and Emmy knew she would need all of the help she could get. By the end of that conversation, she had convinced Cheryl France to not only support the schools, but come out of retirement and run for the position on the board.

"I was done with the schools," Cheryl says. "I had retired and wasn't looking back. But then Emmy and I got to talking, and I saw that she had big plans for Ridgemont; and before I knew it, I had filed my paperwork and was running for the school board."

One down, hundreds more to go.

Still this new superintendent with a lot less experience than drive was convinced that Ridgemont was on the cusp of change. Her time spent talking to the community, hearing what people thought about the schools, their concerns and their hopes was not wasted. Likewise, Emmy was spending time learning what made her staff tick, and their new experiment with service learning spoke to her. Big things—good things—were going to happen. Emmy could feel it.

6

THE ELECTIONEER

Emmy Beeson had stepped into a difficult situation. The Ridgemont district had already put two bond issues on the ballot to build a new school. Both had failed. Another had been considered, but was ultimately removed from the ballot before election day. There were economic considerations, of course. Ridgeway and Mount Victory are rural communities. Money is hard-earned and harder-spent. In a town in which the wealthiest people own land, a bond issue that will tax them more, hits harder than in a suburb made up of quarter-acre lots. And the people who don't own a lot of land already have restrictive means in which to live. That's not to say that every family in the district is cash-strapped or poor. It's just that there's a certain pragmatic perspective that comes with living in such a town.

Then there was the plan.

It had been nearly five decades since the Ridgeway and Mount Victory school districts had merged; but small-town rivalries die hard, if they die at all. The first two ballot proposals were designed around a new K-6 building in Mount Victory and renovations of the Ridgeway building. The buildings had deteriorated so much by the third vote that the plan was for one K-12 building in Mount Victory, where the historic and sentimentally appreciated elementary school had been for over a century. Under the new proposal, the old school in Ridgeway—the junior and high school—would be closed completely, auctioned off and ultimately taken down.

"The way that they usually design schools," Emmy says, "is based on a formula. They plug numbers into a formula—how many first-graders you have, how many second-graders you have, etcetera; and that tells you how much space you need. You need to do these calculations in order to put the issue on the ballot. You have a program." SHP had helped with these calculations programs for both of the previous issues, for the one that was pulled off the ballot and for this third one, as well.

Emmy knew she had her work cut out for her. Her door-to-door brand of politicking would have to be about more than just money, more than economics. She would need to overcome space and time, distance and sentimental values. And that's exactly what she tried to do.

For the first few months in her new position, Emmy, who gleefully admits to knowing little about politics and less about building a school, went from ball game to ball game, church to church and living room to living room, to answer questions, share what the school was doing, ask the congregations to pray for Ridgemont, and plead for the new school.

"People were so attached to the old school," says Sally Henrick, who taught fifth grade in the elementary school in Mount Victory for seven years. "They would drive by and think how beautiful it was."

And it was beautiful. It was the kind of building that makes you think 'they don't make them like that anymore.' Picture perfect. Norman Rockwell perfect. From the outside. But on the inside, Sally says, it was a very different place. "Every time it rained, I would have water coming through my windows." Cold in the winter, hot in the summer, the old elementary school was not the kind of place in which you could imagine students doing their best work. And the Ridgeway junior and senior high was not much better, even if it was, comparatively, newer.

Running an election, particularly one involving new money for a new school, is a complicated business. Ask any superintendent—even those in the allegedly most forward-thinking and progressive school districts—and they will tell you that people are always in favor of better education, but their conviction is often limited to words. And Ridgemont was made even more complicated by the geographical divide of the two communities that it served and the sentimental legacy of the district's history.

It's natural for people to be sentimental about their school, their town and their heritage. These are the building blocks of a cultural identity. Passing the bond issue would mean Ridgeway's losing its foothold in the district. It would mean Mount Victory's losing its historic school building. Even though the problems and realities of the teaching and learning environments were obvious to the district staff and some key influencers in the community, there was not an alternative narrative being told to counteract the riptide forces of legacy and heritage.

Emmy and her staff worked tirelessly. The last ballot issue had been soundly defeated; it went down by more than 300 votes out of around 1,000 votes in the district, a considerable margin. This next campaign meant a lot of convincing, not only of the need, but of Emmy herself, her abilities, the direction of the district.

She spent a lot of time listening, perhaps more than she spent convincing. She heard concerns—about the geographical split, about the nature of education and what the schools were doing to prepare students for life after graduation. Emmy—the first-time administrator, the superintendent who didn't know any better—was getting an on-the-job education in the relationship between a community and its schools.

When, after a marathon sprint toward election day, the polls opened, her impact was clear. The third ballot initiative suffered the same fate as the previous two, but she had closed the margin from a 300-vote trouncing to a 30-vote defeat. It was a moral victory, if not an election win. But while progress had been made, the results were the same. The needs remained, and Emmy was back to square one, back to the drawing board, to a new approach to getting the measure passed and building a future for Ridgemont.

Ridgemont High School opened in 1951, with a gym, locker rooms and additional classrooms added in 1993.

The oldest section of the K-6 Ridgemont Elementary opened in 1912. The gym and cafeteria were added in 1938.

The classrooms in the existing buildings were crowded, had no storage and little daylight.

The classroom conditions in Ridgemont Elementary stifled student and teacher movement.

Ridgemont High School also had overcrowded classrooms as well as heating units that did not work correctly.

Ridgemont Elementary's cafeteria had low ceilings, no windows and very limited space.

The lack of storage space meant the physical education storage was relegated to space on the stage.

The main entrance did not meet accessibility guidelines and presented safety concerns since office workers could not see who entered the building.

The kitchen was very small, offering limited work space and storage.

7

COMMUNITY REFLECTION

SHP Leading Design has long been a leader in community-oriented design. For nearly three decades, the firm has used an approach that allows us to create the best results for students, teachers and the community at large by gathering input early. We don't believe design begins with drawings or calculations. We believe real design begins with a collaborative understanding of a community's priorities: its wants and needs and an understanding of the difference between the two.

We know community involvement and support are the cornerstones of a successful school. By blending the science of research with the art of understanding school district needs, we developed the nationally recognized and award-winning Schoolhouse of Quality process. Our process encourages participation from a wide variety of stakeholders in a number of different ways. We firmly believe it is better to lead with questions, rather than answers and preconceived notions.

Even in a climate in which education seems to be a design-by-numbers environment, we pride ourselves on a passion for making educational environments personal to the communities that they serve. It's reflective of how we think: that despite the headlines and constant talk about standardization, education is not static. It changes. It grows. When it's at its best, it embraces the best ideas and the best tools, to better reach the next generation.

"The general trend is the need to compete," says Todd Thackery, a partner at SHP and the lead planner on the Ridgemont Local School District project. "Teachers and textbooks are no longer the only sources of information. Technology is fundamentally changing how children process information, how teachers teach. It informs the skills that are necessary to compete in a new global economy. School districts are forced to compete with one another, with private schools and alternative learning environments, to attract, retain and prepare students in a constantly shifting environment."

Ridgemont's decision to move away from test-focused teaching was, in many ways, the turning point. It meant a substantial shift toward individualized learning—prioritizing the success of a student over state mandates.

8

THE TURNING POINT

Sitting in her office in the new Ridgemont school, Emmy Beeson is able to smile about what happened after the third ballot push. She, like a survivor looking back at a traumatic event, is able to focus on the silver lining. Their loss on that election day had a cascading effect, all of which enabled her to be sitting in this new office, in this incredible new school. It would not be the school that it is if that vote had gone the other way. She knows that now. But at the time, it seemed doomed. In politics the fourth time is rarely the charm.

Following the tally of that third vote, there were a lot of people in the district—families with young kids—who lost hope, Emmy says. "We had a lot of people who saw the failure of the third vote and thought 'people around here just don't support education,'" she says. "They took their kids and left the district, moved someplace else."

How many? By Ridgemont Local School District standards, quite a lot. In all, around 40 students left. For a large urban or suburban district, that's a rounding error, the usual turnover of families in and out. For Ridgemont, it's a graduating class. And it meant that for the fourth ballot attempt, the math had to be done all over again. The formulas needed to be reworked.

The original plans for the new school were all-inclusive. A K-12 facility in Mount Victory with two gyms, enough space, equipment and facilities to house everything from preschool to senior graduation. However, all of that was based on a certain number of students. Those families packing up their kids and leaving the district for more supportive schools changed the math.

In most school districts, there is strength in numbers. The more students you have, the more families you have, and the more considerations you have. But for Ridgemont, a tiny district by any measure, it turned out to be the opposite.

"We had to rethink the plans," Emmy says. "With fewer students, the needs in the new school changed. We couldn't have two gyms, by the state's calculations.

Fewer students, fewer voters, less budget and an opportunity to rethink a few things. If the new school could only have one gym, could they keep part of the Ridgeway building intact? This would give the district an additional gym, to keep athletics in Ridgeway. What would it mean to keep afterschool and outdoor activities based in Ridgeway, while building the new school in Mount Victory? Did that change the election math?

The district worked with SHP to realign, recalculate and redesign the plan that would inform the bond issue and address the political needs, as well as the practical, instructional needs of the district. "We went back to the calculations," she says. "We went back to the formula."

The new school was designed upon the state-issued design standards based on the smaller enrollment, while the new plan called for maintaining half of the old junior high and high school in Ridgeway. The building would house athletic and outdoor afterschool activities. Half of it would be razed—following an auction of its contents—and the other half would remain an important part of Ridgemont. It wasn't a perfect plan, but Emmy and others hoped it might appease some of the identity and legacy concerns that the voters in Ridgeway might have about losing their school completely.

In the intervening months between the failure of the third issue and the vote on the fourth, more progress had been made toward defining the nature of education at Ridgemont. Service learning was expanding. The agriculture program continued its march toward national prominence. By 2012, the first-time superintendent was beginning to codify a new identity for the district. And the next ballot push would be the true test of the direction that education in Ridgemont was taking. She knew there might not be another shot.

The vote had been so close the last time, it had almost passed. But the previous two had been landslides, and she wasn't sure what would hurt worse: an even tighter election or backwards progress. Administrators more often than not begin their careers as teachers, a role in which they have constant proximity to the impact that schools have on students' lives and achievements. But sometimes the higher a person rises in administration, the more removed he or she becomes from the emotional and intellectual impacts of teaching.

Emmy was not one of those administrators. She wanted to pass the bond issue. On some levels she needed to pass it. It was her first real and public test as a superintendent. She had arrived too late to take charge of the previous election, but this fourth vote? This was on her, and there were a lot of people whom she didn't want to let down.

The district was heading in the right direction. The staff was heading in the right direction. The students were heading in the right direction. She feared that another loss—close or wide—might diminish that progress.

So Emmy, the school board, and key community members and alumni then went back to work rallying community support—ball game by ball game, church by church, living room by living room— this time with a better story to tell. This time there would be a school to support both communities, a plan that fulfilled the needs of both towns, while giving students a better, healthier place to learn. By now service and project-based learning were better established in the district; and Emmy was less of an unfamiliar quantity, a face people knew and, generally, seemed to like.

The effort paid off. On March 6, 2012, the bond issue passed by a vote of 649 - 478, as close to a landslide as small-town elections get and a mandate to build a better school for the students and communities of Ridgeway and Mount Victory.

It was a monumental achievement for Emmy, but marked only the beginning of the work to be done.

9

ENVISIONING RIDGEMONT

Service and project-based learning were clear priorities for the school; and thanks to Stephanie Jolliff's focus on cutting-edge education that was preparing her agricultural students for life after graduation, there was momentum around Ridgemont Local School District. There had been major steps in the right direction, but there was still something missing—a clearly defined mission for the district, something that reflected community values and set the tone for the immediate challenges ahead in the foreseeable future.

SHP had done some really good work in the time since the bond issue passed. We had immersed ourselves in service and project-based learning. We had accounted for the needs of the robust agriculture program. But Emmy Beeson was still curious. She had been a great partner in our process, answering all of the questions that we had, fulfilling every one of our requests with passion and vigor. But there were still questions.

"It started with Stephanie Jolliff's daughters," she says. "They started researching things online. They would email me pictures that they had found and say, 'We really like this couch; we really like this space at this school in Finland.' They are just like their mom, always curious about what's possible, instead of what's likely. I started doing research on my own and with others."

Together with some core staff members, Emmy began look-ing into education around the world and came to the realization that there are no rules. There is only purpose, when it comes to designing a school.

But what Emmy and the Ridgemont staff and stakeholders were doing was something more. It was not simply following our pro-cess to get community involvement; it was taking ownership of the in-tent of the process, in a way that we had seldom experienced before.

"Mission" is a word that is often poorly used. It gets thrown around, bandied about. It becomes something appended to an email signature, a plaque hanging on the wall in the lobby of a building. The mission statement is often seen as a "nice-to-have" or one of those things that gets written down and forgotten about.

When taken seriously, a mission is the result of time spent con-sidering an organization's purpose. It can be a powerful organizing force that helps to heal old wounds, to inform decisions, to clearly articulate the vision that an organization is setting for the future and a means of holding itself accountable to its members and the members yet to come.

Just under the surface of all of the things that had been hap-pening in Ridgemont was a developing sense of purpose—in educa-tion and as a community. There was not a clearly articulated mission, a clear vision for the future in the elections. There were simply needs and legacies and opinions. Emmy realized that, if the new school were going to be built, it would not be built based on physical needs. It had to be built based upon the community's coming together to establish a common vision and a clear mission that would define Ridgemont then and for years to come.

The clock was ticking. After nearly six months of design work since the bond issue passed in March 2012, to get ready for breaking ground on April 6, 2014, Emmy and the leaders of Ridgemont Local School District were now beginning to ask big questions that could have broad and wide-ranging impact on the school. What is the district's mission? What is the community vision for education? What, beyond standardized-test scores and a high graduation rate, were the goals of education in Ridgemont? And how would these questions be answered?

"We had to make a decision," she says. "Were we going to focus on the [standardized] tests, or were we going to prepare students for the world ahead of them? We decided to focus on preparing students for the world that they were likely to be joining. We decided to focus on raising good people. And if we had to choose between raising good people and passing a test, we would take good people."

Of course, it wasn't quite that simple. It never is. But it wasn't especially complicated either. Emmy, needing to rebuild community support around the schools, decided to change the conversations from "what education should be" to "what education could be."

And thus began a community-led initiative designed to capture community priorities, as they related to the schools.

It seems so straightforward and so obvious that the best way to get community buy-in is to ask people what they want. It is, after all, what so much of the world is about. We do research, launch something and test its results. But education, particularly public education, is not an environment known for its adaptability and change.

It is possible to understand what people want. Surveys, polling, community forums and door-to-door canvassing are all ways of gauging how people feel about something. You can put ads in the newspaper, ask people to write letters, have contests and conversations; but all of these techniques are reactive. They are responses to prepared questions. What Emmy and others in Ridgemont needed was something else entirely, a collaborative exploration of the world outside the schools, the world that students were preparing to enter. And it had to happen quickly.

So on January 16, 2013, Emmy and other leaders in the district pulled together community stakeholders, influencers, school leaders and industry experts, to design the future of the district. Attendees included leaders from EDWorks, a subsidiary of the KnowledgeWorks

Foundation; Kathy Meyer and Ellen Erlanger of Partnerships Make a Difference; representatives of the Ohio Department of Education; and the agriculture advocacy group Ohio Growers. Ridgemont was represented by Emmy, of course, but also by the district treasurer, Cheryl France and Board of Education President Corey Ledley, whose agriculture achievements as a student were the catalyst for growth in the program. They were joined by the junior- and senior-high principals; representatives of departments, including physical education, maintenance and administration; and teachers from preschool through high school grade levels. Ridgemont graduates were there, as were leaders from the Ridgeway and Mount Victory communities and businesses.

SHP had three people in attendance, including project leads Todd Thackery, Scott Diesler and Brian Lutz; but our role was not to participate. We were there as silent observers. As a company we have helped to lead a lot of districts through design and construction of buildings, but this day was about the overall objectives of the district and the community that it serves. The invitation foreshadowed the day that was to come:

> *Ridgemont Local School District is thrilled to invite you to a day of envisioning, of dreaming, of grappling with the ideas of educating our students far into the future. As we embark on the design and construction of a new PreK-12 school, we are ever cognizant of how quickly the world is changing around us and how we must be an organization that thrives in the midst of change. We are usually running the race so swiftly that it is not often we can stop long enough to breathe and contemplate all we can be. Today you are invited to contemplate with us as partners in our future.*

Emmy and the leaders of Ridgemont clearly had high expectations for the day, which began with a tour of Battelle, a scientific-research organization based in Columbus. The organization, which serves a wide spectrum of research and manufacturing interests for both scientific and commercial clients, seemed an especially fitting place to begin the day, as the kind of hands-on, real-world application of science and technology practiced there represented the post-grad-uation world for which many Ridgemont students were bound.

Partners in Innovation, including SHP Leading Design, were then asked to share their vision for the future of education and what kinds of opportunities and challenges face students today and in the near future. The tour, the presentations—all were a prelude to an af-ternoon session of dreaming and imagining, of challenging the status quo and setting the tone for Ridgemont as a district.

"It was thrilling to be there," says Ellen. "You see a lot of schools incorporate programs like service learning and multidisciplinary stud-ies into their curriculum. But what happened with Ridgemont was dif-ferent. They decided to make those things central to their approach to education."

Even three years later, Emmy looks back on the day as a turn-ing point for education in her district. Her report delivered to the school board a week later, on January 23, 2013, sums it up best:

On January 16, 2013, Ridgemont Local School District embarked on a landmark day, which would alter the path of the district for generations to come. Teachers, administration, businesspeople, graduates and representatives from the education community at large met to share thoughts on the future of education and more specifically the future of education at Ridgemont. Speakers from EDWorks, Partnerships Make a Difference, the Ohio Department of Education and Ohio Growers presented from their perspectives and urged the district to consider real-world connections, reinvention of the industrial delivery model of education and customized education, based on student needs.

When the group sat collectively to investigate the items pre-sented, ideas such as business partnerships, solving real-world problems, blended learning, education that exists anywhere and anytime, community connections and flexible student scheduling came to the forefront. Ultimately the collaborative team decided on three focuses that will guide the district as they continue through the building process. These three concepts will also be the framework from which the district will build its mission and vision for the next century of educating students.

1. Service and project-based learning that addresses real-world problems for real-world audiences

2. Customized student learning, based on student need and readiness, which uses technology as a primary tool

3. Deeper, amplified learning that makes numbers 1 and 2 purposeful and meaningful to students

"We were future-stating," Emmy says. "We started with the idea that there are no limits. We challenged everything from grade levels to technology and based everything on service and project-based learning."

It's ambitious, to say the least, for a superintendent to make a statement about the principles that will guide how a district will approach education over time frames marked not by months or years, but by decades. Even more astounding is the near universal support from the board of education that followed.

The board called Ridgemont's new approach "Designing the Future"; and a single statement, a statement that follows the signature on Emmy's emails, that resonates through the halls of the Ridgemont school and seems encoded into the very DNA of the community, defined it. Here it is:

"In Designing the Future, Ridgemont Local School District will create partnerships with our families and community that broaden minds to learn and serve through collaboration, innovation and rigorous academics for life's learning journey."

There's nothing ambiguous about that statement. There is nothing aspirational. It is a declaration of intent, a promise made by a school system and upheld by a community. Learning at Ridgemont in the days and weeks following the Envisioning Day and in all the days and weeks to come would be fundamentally changed.

"We decided that day that we were going to focus on educating good people," Emmy says, "people who are prepared to take on challenges, who love learning, who feel a sense of responsibility for enriching and serving their community. We decided that we were not going to mark student success and achievement by traditional methods. Instead, we were going to mark success by creating better people."

Better people, good people. It's not often that you hear those kinds of words in a conversation about student achievement from a superintendent. Too often achievement is marked by test scores or graduation rates. But maybe it took a small community and the vision of a rare leader to change the conversation.

There would be practical considerations, of course. An emphasis on collaborative teaching across multiple subjects simultaneously would require a different approach to design. And an emphasis on project-based and service learning would require different kinds of spaces for students to gather, to work independently or in small groups. There was also the matter of longevity. The school would need to be adaptable not only in the short term, but over the long haul too. Ridgemont was making a declaration that its approach to education would neither be static nor become stale. The district was going to attempt to move at the pace of change in the real world—a challenge for businesses, an Everest for most school districts (for which change is iterative and slow).

But by the end of the day on January 16, 2013, all of the bubbling notions, all of the fits and starts toward a new way of teaching and learning had become codified. Ridgemont now had a clear focus for what was to come. They would use this over the next year to meet with 100 stakeholders, to explore the core business of education at Ridegemont. The result would be a vison and mission, a directional system to lead the district. The community came together in a way that few communities have before and decided together what mattered the most.

With design principles in hand, Emmy returned to her small, cinderblock office in the old school in Ridgeway, excited and a bit overwhelmed. The vision was there. Now all that she needed was buy-

in from her staff, students and the rest of the community.
And, of course, a new school.

10

CHANGE OF PLANS

_____

The Envisioning Day had been a tremendous success, if a bit overwhelming. This notion of Designing the Future, coupled with the challenge of making education irresistible, was exhilarating for Emmy Beeson and the others who had attended, but it also raised some questions about the proposed school design. Having no experience in building a school, Emmy wondered what it would mean to incorporate the new vision and mission of the schools into the physical structures and how the two things would work with and enable each other.

She wasn't the only one.

Todd Thackery had been there that day, but only as an observer," Emmy says. "He hadn't participated, but I saw him making notes and sketches the whole time. The next day I was in a core team meeting, and Todd said, 'We haven't designed the right school for you. We need to do a redesign.'"

Emmy's heart sank. She knew he was right, but how could it be? The staff had already spent six months working with SHP and the community to create the current designs. How could she ask the staff to start over? How could she break the news?

Like so many times throughout this process, it was Stephanie Jolliff who provided the answer. She was the first person with whom

Emmy spoke after talking to Todd about the redesign, and she assured the superintendent that everything would be okay.

"We had a professional-development day the next day anyway, which meant that the staff would be in the building, but there would be no students around," Emmy recalls. "Stephanie and I talked in her classroom, and she said she was on it."

She grabbed another teacher, and they went around the district one by one, explaining the situation to the staff and convincing them that the redesign was the way to go. "Stephanie and [another teacher] Darcy went rogue," Emmy says. "I sat in my office going crazy; but at the end of the day, they came back and said, 'It's done; let's do this.'"

Whether it was the respect that she has earned as an educator or sheer force of will, Stephanie managed to convince the staff at Ridgemont that the redesign was in their best interest, that it would serve the students and community better to build a school based upon the newly minted community vision.

"At the end of the day, I called Todd back and told him to go for it," Emmy says. There's a sense of awe and more than a little discomfort that comes through her voice when she recalls the moment. It's as if she still can't believe it happened.

We recognized right away that Ridgemont's new vision called for a new approach to the built environment, one that was in line with our vision for education, based upon our six attributes of individual learning. Out of the collaborative exploration that took place during the Envisioning Day, we were able to imagine whole new ways of educating and preparing students for the 21st century and beyond.

"It was a challenge, to be sure," says Todd. "We understood how to incorporate a community's needs into design, but this forced us to stretch, to think in terms of priorities and sort of abandon the rules."

No "cells and bells," but rather a collaborative project- and service-learning environment, one that truly and completely prepared students for a world beyond the classroom, a world in which technology was incorporated into work, not relegated to a computer lab; a place in which students not only worked at individualized paces, but took ownership of their learning. These were not challenges that could be solved by equation. These were challenges that required a designer to fundamentally question everything they knew about creating spaces for minds to grow. And in so doing, it would force Emmy, her staff and the school board to change the way that they brought the community into the process, to explain a whole new concept in time for the beginning of construction.

The school needed to be redesigned around a few key principles established in the Envisioning Day. First and foremost, the building needed to be flexible, to accommodate a new emphasis on team cross-discipline instruction. Where traditional approaches might dictate subject- or purpose-dedicated spaces, Ridgemont's mission of integrated learning meant that spaces had to be more flexible and appropriate for separate uses than other more traditional models. A team of teachers combining English, social studies and technology may have different needs on different days, in terms of space, depending upon that day's content curriculum.

And with a clear emphasis on project-based and service learning, there was a previously unmet need for incorporating spaces designed for student-to-student collaboration. Meeting in hallways or other spaces would not be feasible. It might be fine for a school in which projects were an occasional part of learning, but student projects would be central to Ridgemont's educational approach. Students needed spaces that could adapt to collaborations of different sizes—spaces to work alone, to work with teachers in small groups and to mentor each other.

Designing Ridgemont would mean thinking beyond calculations and design principles. We needed to create a new approach to bring students together, in order to enable learning, to make our vision for the building as strong as the community's vision for education.

We went back to drawing board, quite literally. Over the course of two weeks, we put together a new design to deliver a future-focused learning environment, flexible enough to support the kind of collaboration needed for the new approach to teaching, while still providing enough structure to keep students on track.

We incorporated extended learning areas, basically small-group and individual workspace for students, as well as teachers, who would also have a common planning area; but in the junior and high school areas, teachers would not be assigned classrooms. They would collaborate and plan together in large office spaces. We re-envisioned the media center to become a book lounge, complete with school store, which would be run by students as part of their service-learning program, and put movable walls into nearly every classroom, to accommodate team and interdisciplinary teaching at every grade level.

After the initial design push, students even got the chance to share their ideas. Math students applied their geometry lessons to concept outdoor learning spaces. Elementary-school students gave design direction for a custom playground. Staff inputs were free-flowing. Stephanie's vision for the vocational and agricultural learning area was crucial.

The experience of working so closely with the community and its vision for what education can and should look like pushed our staff to challenge conventional thinking at every turn. And the result was a design for an 88,838-square-foot school much different than originally planned. The only thing standing between Ridgemont and a more fully realized vision for the future was construction—and the work that Emmy needed to do in order to get everyone else on the staff and in the community on board.

11

BUYING IN

With the bond issue passed, the new school designed and a new vision for the district in hand, Emmy Beeson still faced challenges in bringing about broad change in Ridgemont Local School District. Many staff members had been teaching "the old way" for most of their careers. Many members of the community were still unsure about how Designing the Future would work. Students too had to have had some doubts, particularly the older ones.

Some battles had been won, but creating systemic change would require continued diligence and investment from Emmy, the district, the staff and everyone involved.

Service-learning, along with team and interdisciplinary teaching, in particular, needed to be expanded within the district prior to the move into the new school, both of which required professional development and expanded resources for teachers, as they made the transition.

"Many districts will experiment with project-based learning; but few offer the support required, in terms of continuing training and making adjustments to teacher and student schedules, to make it a success," says Ellen Erlanger, of Partnerships Make a Difference. "Emmy did everything possible before the school was built to get her staff ready for the transition." She hired half-day subs for teachers who needed training. She changed the schedule on two days of the week, to accommodate teachers' planning together. She helped lead the charge to make student projects more visible to the community at large.

Of course, not all of the staff was completely on board with the changes. Many were hesitant to adopt and change. "At first, we decided not to focus on 100 percent adoption," says Emmy. "We instead let people raise their hands; and when they did, we provided necessary resources, in terms of time and training and freedom to develop plans together."

The old guard would be the old guard. Every year the small district loses nearly a quarter of its staff. As such, recruitment is a constant need in the district, and the new vision even changed the way in which Emmy and the school board evaluated potential candidates. Less emphasis was placed on resumes, and more discussion on philosophy and mission were had with potential candidates than might have taken place in the past. Could this person adapt to a service-learning environment? Were they open to interdisciplinary and team-teaching approaches? Could they handle working in a school that would be unlike any school they had ever been in?

"I had one candidate come in for a math position," Emmy says. "He was very qualified and clearly a very good teacher. We talked for a while, and I asked him what he thought—whether he thought he could adjust to our vision. He told me how exciting it all seemed, but admitted that, no, he didn't think he could. That was fine. That was okay. It was better to know now than to find out that it was the wrong fit later."

That was the general approach to gaining staff buy-in to the district's vision—allowing them to search within themselves, to judge for themselves whether or not they would be a fit. No mandates, no prescriptions. The train was moving, but all who wanted to board were welcome. By the time the 2014-15 school year came around, many members of the staff were taking ownership of the vision for themselves.

"I remember sitting in a professional-development meeting with other administrators and teachers," Emmy says. "One of our math teachers was explaining to other teachers in our county how she team-taught subjects across grade levels with another teacher. At some point she saw me and had a look like 'we never asked if that was okay or got permission.' But of course, it was okay. It was great. They were taking initiative without being asked. I loved it."

Cheryl France says that changes were happening in the community during the intervening years between the writing of the design principles and the completion of the school. She knows everything there is to know about Ridgemont and the community that it serves, and she began to see changes in student performance and community sentiment. She said that people began to forget (or at least ignore) old rivalries and scars, and instead a sense of curiosity started to grow. People became interested in what was happening. The schools' importance to the community began to take a new shape.

"Success is contagious," says Eric Hill. He too serves on the board of education, including as president. His mom had been on the board of education. He grew up in the community. He graduated from Ridgemont, class of 1986. He and his family moved away when the district was flagging and stale, but returned, hoping to be a part of making things better. "When I came back in 2003, I got a sense that the attitude toward the schools was that they were 'good enough.' Why expect more? But then all of this started happening. You saw teachers and students taking on bigger ideas; you saw a vision coming into focus. You start to see success, and it becomes irresistible. It's empowering. You want to be a part of it."

Emmy was charged with supporting her staff, to help them see what education could look like on a daily basis within the walls of their new learning organization; and she was charged with truly hearing the community, to be sure that Ridgemont's values reflected those outside of its walls. This process of creating Ridgemont's directional system began with the Envisioning Day in January 2013, but it didn't end there. From that meeting Emmy and her principals began meeting with focus groups, to ask them what they believed the core business of their school should be. "Educating students" was not allowed. Emmy says, "That was a given. Every school would say that. We needed to know what made us different from the schools around us. What would give us our identity?"

Focus groups with students, parents, community members, alumni, teachers and staff members were held. In a district with only 1,000 voters, Emmy and her team met with over 100 individuals. From these meetings came their vision of Designing the Future and their mission statement. These two anchors attached to their design principles from the Envisioning Day. And these pillars birthed their six district instructional strategies and the "Gopher Traits" (a mascot-inspired name for those character traits to be exhibited by all students and staff at Ridgemont). Over the course of three years, with more exploration, conversation and reinvention, the district also committed to a core set of beliefs and defined its partnerships. All of these concepts come together to form its directional system.

Ridgemont now has an identity. Emmy can tell you why they do or do not do things. Everything must be aligned to the directional system. The board of education can tell you why they do or do not do things. Everything must align to the directional system. This is not a mission statement that gets dusty sitting on a shelf, but the heartbeat of the organization.

With staff buy-in and a community-driven direction in place, students were changing, as well. Stephanie Jolliff and Apryl Ealy say that they saw students being willing to take more risks. "I told my students, if they had an idea, to try it; and if it fails, we'll fix it," says Stephanie. "Teaching isn't scripted; it's improvised. We adapt and change. We learn from what works and what doesn't. I think this new vision and the support that came with it helped us instill that same sort of thinking in our students."

Success was increasingly defined not by having the right answer, but by helping kids understand the value in attempting something, in trying something and failing. The definition of success, from a student's perspective, was changing from being right to being un-afraid to fail. "It's okay for kids to fail," says Cheryl, the retired teacher. "Just not to quit—and kids were not as quick to quit as they used to be."

While the educational manifestation was taking root in the classrooms in Mount Victory and Ridgeway, the physical embodiment of it was taking shape on 40 acres of donated farmland in Mount Victory.

Constructing a school is a complicated business. There are a lot of moving parts. But Emmy knew that the closer she could bring the community, staff and students to the project, the greater the excitement for its completion would be. She began taking groups of students through the construction site weekly and hosting regular Thursday-night tours for anyone in the community—or those interested in the project from elsewhere—so they could begin to see and understand how the building would help enable the district's vision.

"I would call the construction managers and tell them I was bringing people over for a tour," Emmy says. "They always seemed a little confused, so I asked how people normally handle tours on a construction site. They told me most people don't ask to lead tours; but I didn't know any better, and it seemed like the right thing to do."

If there were one sentence that described Emmy's leadership through this whole ordeal—two elections, two school designs, the development of a district directional system, training teachers in that vision and making the community feel a part of the project—it would be the previous one: "I didn't know any better, and it seemed like the right thing to do."

Emmy doesn't operate from a perspective of rules and following them. She operates from a perspective of desired outcomes and trying everything possible to manifest those outcomes. Through it all, through two years of construction following two years of election and design, she focused on desired outcomes and sought to build consensus in how to approach achieving them.

By the spring of 2015, it felt like a milestone was just around the corner. The school building was set to be open for the first day of school in August, when the district has traditionally begun the school year. But there's a tradition in rural districts like Ridgemont affecting school programming. The first day of school was scheduled for August 24. Had things gone according to plan, students would have arrived for the first day of school and spent a week being students. The school would have then closed for the Hardin County Fair, when many students would be busy displaying projects or working to keep the event going. They would return to school in early or mid-September, to resume the academic year.

But things did not go as planned. In any major construction project, there are bound to be unexpected things that pop up to challenge the deadline. Small construction delays meant that the first day at the school would not take place until September 14, 2015. Always cool under pressure, always seeking to build community buy-in, Emmy reached out to staff, students, parents, the community at large and anyone else who might have been interested, to let them know personally how the delays had impacted the schedule. And to put the community's minds at ease, she scheduled an open house for the first night of school.

It just seemed like the right thing to do.

12

A NEW BEGINNING

Emmy Beeson has given a lot of tours of the new building. Weekly when it was under construction; and since it opened officially in September 2015, she has led tours for parents, teachers, board members, staff and visitors—even superintendents from districts as far away as the Pennsylvania border and beyond. "I never get tired of giving tours," she says. "I'm just so excited about this school and this opportunity. I'm really proud to be a part of what's happening at Ridgemont."

And the school is indeed an exciting extension of Ridgemont Local School District's vision. It feels modern, but warm. Visitors have joked that walking through the new school is like walking through an IKEA catalog. Furniture is modular, mobile and comfortable. Everything in the building is designed to move, to adapt, to adjust, to encourage collaboration and communication.

"I do not think the furniture will ever be in the place that it was set for the first day of school again," says Todd Thackery. He looks at the project, improbable as it was, following three failed levies and a complete redesign on an almost inconceivably tight timeline, as an accomplishment. In fact, everyone at SHP understands that Ridgemont has altered what we might have believed possible before the work began.

When leading a tour, Emmy takes visitors to the elementary wing first, showing them the classrooms with operating walls that allow teachers the flexibility to team teach. Team teaching allows teachers to help students move at the pace that they need, without disrupting the overall progress of the class. In those elementary rooms are smaller conference rooms for specialized instruction, something that was once relegated to the hallway. Students who need extra help no longer need to leave the classroom and can get the instruction that they need without disturbing the rest of the class. Giant windows face outside, allowing natural light to flood the rooms.

On the interior wall of each class is an oversized glass garage door that comes down from the ceiling to countertop height. The doors can be raised, and stools on both sides of the counter help to create a unique collaboration space.

"The high school students volunteer to come down here and work with the elementary kids," she says. "The counter is made of whiteboard, so the kids can work together closely and explore lessons together."

The elementary classrooms are, of course, equipped with smartboards and other technology, to help teachers facilitate 21st-century learning. But perhaps the most modern features of the elementary wing are the nontraditional learning spaces in the central gathering space in which the rooms meet. There are comfortable chairs for students to read in, tables to work on and a massive, two-story window that looks out toward the playground and acres of school-owned, undeveloped property beyond. "This is the best view in the whole school," Emmy says. "The kids are all on their best behavior in the classrooms, because they want to be rewarded with time in this space, time to read and work independently."

On the other side of the massive window is an outdoor classroom designed with inspiration and contribution from Ridgemont students. "They were in high school math at the time, and they took it on as part of their project-based learning to apply their math lessons to design an outdoor classroom. They worked with the landscape architects from SHP to create this space," Emmy says. A set of small benches faces the glass. Students can sit there or elsewhere in the area, while the teacher makes notes, draws pictures or writes questions on the glass.

The natural world, in addition to being a key part of our emphasis on sustainability, is also very important to the students at Ridgemont. Many of them come from agricultural families, they spend time outside, they play outside, and they help out around the farm. Perhaps nowhere is this more evident than in the student-inspired custom playground. "The fourth grade students wanted the playground to be natural. They chose natural colors. They designed the slides to represent rivers and gave the site a treehouse look," Emmy says. "They are incredibly proud of that playground."

Upstairs Emmy leads tours through the junior-high wing, where student lockers line the interior walls and floor-to-ceiling windows bring the hallways into the classrooms. In every class students move plush chairs and desks, tables and stools to get comfortable.

She greets students in the hall, compliments them on their work. She walks to the humanities classroom, where students are working—some at desks, some in a U-shaped couch configuration, some independently, some getting more personal attention from one of the two teachers who have teamed up for the year. "We used to teach English and social studies and technology," she says. "But now we teach humanities. There was a lot of overlap in what students were learning in English and in social studies that the teachers got together and combined. We used to teach technology, but that didn't seem to make sense anymore. Instead, we've incorporated technology into learning other subjects. We don't teach classes on pencils and paper. Why would we do it for technology?"

This freedom for teachers to be proactive, to team up without being assigned and to explore new ways of teaching, new ways for students to learn is core to the mission of Ridgemont's Designing the Future vision. Some teachers were proactive in the last year at the old school and began team teaching without seeking (or gaining) preapproval from the board. Others have been a bit more hesitant to adapt. And still others have come to Ridgemont expressly for the opportunity to break new ground in education, like the new math teacher in the district who left a tenured job elsewhere to pursue new thinking, without so much as a pay raise.

The seventh- to 12th-grade wing of the school can be completely reconfigured based upon student and teacher need, and different classrooms and spaces offer different environments. While one classroom is best for lecturing, another is better for group work and so on.

"Every wall that is not load-bearing is either movable, able to be raised or made of drywall," Emmy says. "That way if, in 20 years our needs change, we can reconfigure just about everything." The district is working on a system that will allow teachers the flexibility to move classes depending upon the priorities for the day, but one step at a time. For now, she says, she's just thrilled to see teachers taking ownership of the space proactively.

The math classroom on the first floor is another manifestation of the Ridgemont vision. Three teachers have teamed up to teach nearly 50 students at a time together. The students still receive the personal attention that they need, while progressing through the coursework at an even pace. This kind of teaching and student-centric learning would never have been possible in the old schools. Indeed, there are few schools in the country that can accommodate such a forward-thinking approach, and it's garnering attention for the district.

"Honestly, I was happy in my old position," says Sally Henrick. "I had that school running like a well-oiled machine. But I heard about what was happening here, and I wanted to be a part of it." Sally is the curriculum principal for K-12 at Ridgemont. Every old model of how schools are run is being tested there, including administration. While tradition would dictate that even a combined school has separate principals for elementary and secondary education, Ridgemont has, instead, divided the responsibility by areas of focus. Sally leads curriculum, while another principal is focused on student life: service learning, project-based learning, discipline and extracurricular activities. This new job is Sally's second stint with Ridgemont, where she taught fifth grade for seven years in the pre-Emmy days. She says the job is unique, in that it's without precedent, and makes comparisons of what's happening in the district with the kind of hacker thinking that separates Silicon Valley's approach from other industries.

Sally credits Emmy with the change, which is a little intimidating, but exciting. "It's so strange," Emmy says. "I read about new things being tested in districts around the world and think 'we're doing that right here in Hardin County.' It's incredible to think that Ridgemont is doing these things."

Everywhere you look on one of Emmy's tours of the school, you see new thinking. Whether it's the area near the cafeteria that has replaced a traditional library with a Barnes & Noble-esque cafe featuring shelves of books or the music room behind the cafeteria that can be converted into an auditorium stage by moving a curtain and sliding a wall, there are signs of innovative thinking built upon experience. Common areas on each of the floors connect classroom spaces; and meeting rooms have been rethought to become student offices, where students can work quietly on projects without leaving the watchful eye of teachers, thanks to the glass walls that provide quiet order without separation.

If the true heart of Ridgemont is anywhere, it's on the first floor of the high school, just off the student-designed outdoor classroom. This is the agriculture classroom, the domain of Stephanie Jolliff and her renowned students. The classroom itself is covered in awards and other evidence of the incredible achievements. On the door, in black lettering are Stephanie's name and some of her credits: Ohio Agriculture Woman of the Year, Ohio VFW Teacher of the Year, Ohio Association of Agricultural Educators President.

But the real credit is what happens inside the classroom. On a tour in December 2015, Emmy pokes her head into the classroom just as students are tallying the latest results from an annual fruit sale to support the FFA program at Ridgemont. "Mrs. Beeson," Stephanie says, "I thought you might want to know that the students have officially crossed the $40,000 mark in this year's fruit sale."

It's an astounding number, tallied in a student-created Excel spreadsheet that is projected on the wall by a smartboard. Emmy congratulates them; but the 20 or so students are hard at work on other things, so the tour continues into the massive and pristine agriculture laboratory. Imagine a wood shop, but much nicer, bigger and more technologically advanced than anything that you might picture. Two-story ceilings, vented workstations, technology to learn and explore new techniques in growing crops, and the hands-on experience of growing a business are just some of the features of the lab, which even we at SHP had to see to really believe. Attached is a greenhouse, to support year-round growing, learning and experimenting. It's in this room that the vision of preparing students for life after graduation becomes reality. While every room, every space, nook and area of the school is designed to foster student achievement, the agriculture room and lab are designed to create excellence in an area vital to the community.

Agriculture is one of the world's largest industries. And unlike the agriculture of generations past, growing crops today is driven by a mixture of experience and technology. Ridgemont and Stephanie are determined to educate a better class of agriculture professionals, to prepare students for the reality of modern farming and production, and give them a love of learning and exploring that will serve them for their entire career and beyond.

It takes a special kind of teacher and a special kind of community to make that kind of educational priority more than just lip service. And for nearly a decade, Stephanie and Ridgemont did more than could be expected with what they had. But this new learning environment will allow students to break new ground in agricultural learning, something that companies like Monsanto and Bayer Crop Science have noticed. Ridgemont students will enjoy a world-class education, extraordinary opportunities in industry and unprecedented access to facilities, to give them a leg up when graduation comes around.

Emmy continues the tour, stopping at the energy-efficient kitchen, where the staff has the space and facilities to provide meals for students like they never had before in the old schools. She opens the teacher meeting room/lunch space and the mechanical area, where she recites impressive stats about the geothermal heating and cooling system, which includes 72 wells, each 450 feet deep, and more than 13 miles of piping, to maintain even temperatures throughout the school without wasting energy. It's a far cry from the old schools, in which rain came through windows and drafts were the norm.

When she steps into the gym, the lights and HVAC system turn on, thanks to motion-sensing controls. It's the only place in the whole school that the district's colors—green and gold—are central to the decor. Throughout the rest of the school, natural earth tones and softer colors liven up the sunlit environments. But in the gym, where the basketball games are played, school spirit mattered. "Colors were very important to us," she says. "In so many schools, the colors of the sports teams are everywhere. We wanted the rest of the school to be about learning, about bringing the outside in. But in the gym, we thought it was an appropriate place to put our pride on display."

Everywhere you turn on one of Emmy's tours, pride is on display. Student artwork is mounted for public enjoyment; students work together in common areas, learning and completing projects. Older students mentor younger ones, helping them with their lessons, yes, but also setting the tone for what is expected of a Ridgemont student —leadership, collaboration, respect for one another and a passion for learning.

Emmy concludes the tour near the two-story entrance and the front office. It's clear that she is incredibly proud of the school. We all are. But what's even clearer is that, despite the breakthroughs in design and the long road to the finished construction, the work to be done at Ridgemont is far from over. "We're really just getting started," she says. "The building is a massive step, but we have a lot of work to do before we can say we've achieved our vision."

The media center has been re-envisioned as a smaller book lounge and collaboration zone with a coffee shop and spirit wear area. The space has the flexibility for lectures, as well.

The tall ceilings, large windows, and a variety of seating choices deliver an inviting cafeteria space.

The elementary classrooms offer the flexibility to support team teaching.

Large windows in the art room showcase creativity at work.

Elementary classrooms open to Extended Learning Areas (ELAs), which are large enough to hold two to three classes.

Open stairways, large windows and natural elements and color create a welcoming small group learning space.

With windows and acoustic panels, the stage doubles as the band room.

The new entrance meets accessibility guidelines and allows administration staff to clearly see all who enter and exit the building.

The seventh- through 12th-grade classrooms can be reconfigured as needed.

Double doors and plenty of glass in the seventh-through 12th-grade wings create transparency from the classrooms to the ELAs.

A small group area off the ELA is designed for small group work and individualized study.

A courtyard offers seating for students and faculty to enjoy the outside.

Spaces were designed with the student in mind—from charging stations and seating variety, to large windows that provide plenty of natural light.

The garage doors in the elementary learning areas support class collaboration when opened. Plenty of storage in the Extended Learning Areas leaves more space in the classrooms for students and teachers movement.

Dedicated lab space support the school's various career tech programs, ranging from Agricultural Education to woodshop and welding.

13

THE FUTURE
OF RIDGEMONT

At the time that this book is being written, the students and staff of Ridgemont Local School District have been in the new school for two academic years. It's too early to know the impact of the new facility: too soon to know how a fully collaborative and service-based approach to learning is affecting grades; too soon to understand how interdisciplinary teaching is affecting student readiness for life after high school or staff satisfaction, or whether or not it even will.

There are no metrics that account for the kinds of decisions that the leaders in Ridgemont made. There is no standardized test for community orientation or a student's sense of responsibility in being a solution to challenges facing their town, their school and their family. There is only observation...for now, at least.

In his book *How We Got to Now*, Steven Johnson argues that measurement is a key driver in innovation. He writes that "new ways of measuring create new ways of making" and cites examples like a scientist's ability to measure the impact of bacteria on the human body from a microscopic level as the enabling factor in stopping the rampant spread of cholera. Breakthroughs in measurement have been the backbone of everything from manufacturing—allowing three-dimensional scans to be translated into three-dimensional printing—to the items that Amazon thinks you might like to add to your basket, through measurement-driven recommendation algorithms.

Johnson's argument is true in many cases, but not in all. In some cases innovation is born from vision, and measurement is left to catch up. That seems to be the case with Ridgemont. The vision for active, engaging, solutions-oriented education precedes standards or, at the very least, surpasses them.

"The students who learn through service learning are still learning the same content that they might need to cover to pass a standardized test," says Kathy Meyer, of Partnerships Make a Difference. "But they learn at a deeper level, an emotional level. They learn to connect those lessons with real-world application that is relevant to their immediate lives."

They learn better, deeper, longer-lasting lessons that will stick with them in a way that memorizing a formula or grammatical rules never could. So when Ridgemont adopted the Designing the Future platform as its mission, it was not dismissing the notion of measuring student performance the old-fashioned way. The people there were simply thinking beyond it.

"If we do this the right way, we should see improvement in student test scores and overall academic performance," says Emmy Beeson. "There's research out there that indicates that will happen. It's not that we are no longer participating in things like standardized testing; it's just that we are choosing not to focus on them."

Every student at Ridgemont, which already has a graduation rate higher than 95 percent, is expected to take one of three paths when they leave the schools: go to college or some sort of advanced education, join the military or join the workforce in a meaningful way. All three of those outcomes are desirable. All three will be markers of student success. The district will measure its success by its ability to prepare those students to not only follow those paths, but excel in them; to leave Ridgemont with the best practical and theoretical education that they could have hoped for, a sense of community, real-world application of knowledge and a lifelong love of learning. "Those are things that a test score can't tell you," says Sally Henrick, the K-12 principal in charge of curriculum. "Those are the vital outcomes of education that you just can't see in a number."

Emmy and Sally say that the district is working on a new measurement standard designed specifically for the values outlined in the Designing the Future mission statement. The Education Quality Index will take into account a student's academic achievement, of course, but also their community impact and their success after leaving Ridgemont. It won't be easy, but change never is. And if working with Emmy Beeson for the last few years has taught us anything, it is that nothing is impossible; it simply hasn't been done before.

So if direct measurement of achievement is still some time off in the future, how do those most closely associated with the Ridgemont vision think the school has impacted student life? Well, Kathy and Ellen Erlanger, also of Partnerships Make a Difference, say that the impact of service learning is evident every day, in every corner of the school. Whether it is high school students mentoring elementary-school kids during free periods or math students working together with Stephanie Jolliff's vocational-agriculture students to design, plan and build outdoor furniture for the playground, there is an air of collaboration—of learning being a subset of something bigger and simultaneously more and less tangible—that a visitor to the school can sense the moment they walk through the doors.

It's visible in the three students sitting in the high school student offices, planning the next phases of a project. It's visible in the students gathered around Chromebook computers, entering data into a spreadsheet about a fundraising drive. It's visible in the student artwork on display throughout the school. It's visible in the staff, which has surpassed even Emmy's expectations in how they have adapted to and adopted the Ridgemont vision.

"We expected that there would be some uneasiness when we moved into the new school," she says. "The last year in the old buildings was kind of a trial run for how we wanted things to work in the new school. We saw some staff members taking ownership back then, and we expected that others might be slow to adopt once we moved. But that hasn't been the case. We haven't seen any people waiting on the sidelines. Some might be diving in deeper than others; but in general, I'd say that those staff who are here seem to want to be here, want to be part of what we're doing."

Again, time will tell. Older students, juniors and seniors the year the school opened, had the hardest time with the change—the freedom, the movement, the openness of it all. Some seniors have confessed to Emmy that they felt like they had moved out of the district in which they had spent their entire lives, so jarring was the transition. But the vast majority, particularly the younger students, seems to be adapting beyond expectation.

"We knew going into this that it was a big experiment," says Emmy. "We were either going to succeed wildly or fail miserably. There was no in between. We were either going to fundamentally change our values and stick to it, or we would go down in flames. It was and still is a big risk." But, as the motto for the British Special Air Service reminds us, "He who dares, wins."

Sally's daring was particularly emblematic of the type of draw that Ridgemont's vision has on educators looking for a different way of doing things, those teachers yearning to put their ideas to work, to try new approaches and to go beyond the standards set for them. She was an elementary principal in another district not far from Ridgemont, but living in Mount Victory when the ballot issue passed. She was not a part of the design process, the Envisioning Day workshop or even the intervening years during which Emmy was leading the district toward adoption of the new approach. Instead, she was a community resident with a comfortable job that she had worked hard to make her own. But it was the notion of teaching beyond the tests, of daring to try something different that brought her back to the district in which she had taught for seven years.

"This is scary," she says. "There is no template for my job. In my old school, I had everything down to a system. I was in control. Here, well, I've never been a K-12 principal in charge of curriculum before.

I've never been a co-principal before. Every day I come in, and I face challenges that I could never have imagined.

"But," she continues, "I kept seeing all of the things that they were trying here. I kept learning more about the service and project-based learning, the interdisciplinary studies, things that I had only ever read about in educational-leadership magazines. And I couldn't believe these things were happening here in my own community. I had to be a part of it."

That type of freedom with a purpose, that sense of exploration and accountability for many educators is too much. They have enough to deal with. There are enough challenges just trying to get kids to learn, let alone making learning meaningful and dynamic. Taking on such pressures willingly will ruin a teacher or administrator, Sally says. "I hate to think of what any one of us would do if we ever left here. I think we're all going to be ruined by it, spoiled. After just a short time back here, I don't know how I could ever work anywhere else."

And how the students have adapted, how they've taken on a different kind of learning, has echoed through the district and impressed the superintendent. "I had a student tell me that they were working on a group project and wanted to stay at school, but couldn't," Emmy says. "They had to go home; so one of the students set up a Google Hangout, so they could keep working from home. These are elementary-school students, and they are totally engaged. It's the kind of thing that you could never have dreamed of, if we'd kept doing things the old way."

As for Emmy, she says that the five years leading up to the opening of the new school were a marathon and a sprint, both arduous and gone in the blink of an eye. But she's not resting on the laurels or accomplishments of the past.

She continues to take a Silicon Valley hacker's approach to finding better solutions to the everyday challenges of life in the new school. Like how she changed the school schedule on Mondays and Tuesdays, in order to provide (and mandate) time for teachers to sit together and plan. Or how she manages the pressures of adapting to a new building with new spaces and rules, while managing to be thoughtful and articulate with the superintendents from across the state and beyond who have heard about Ridgemont and want to get a better look at how it works. She has even created a directional system for the building, a document to codify and instruct future teachers, staff and students in the principles that guided the design and the intention behind them, to manifest what's expected to happen in the building long after she and others are gone.

There's almost too much to think about to take a break. She's clearly proud of the school. She's proud of the district. She's proud of her staff and students. She obviously takes a tremendous amount of pride in what they have been able to accomplish here. But she can't sit still, can't fade into the background, because one day she won't be there. Whether its 20 years from now and she's settled into a life of retirement or three years from now when life pulls her away, there will come a time when she won't be there, when Stephanie, who has been working toward her PhD and lecturing at universities and agricultural conferences around the country and the world, won't be there. And the vision set by the district cannot be hung on the heads of the people who wrote it; it cannot die with their departure.

"My focus now is on expanding and sustaining," she says. "I'm working with the board of education, to train them on how to hire the right kinds of people to make this work. I'm working on putting in place the systems necessary to support the kind of learning that we want to happen here."

She's working on defining and redefining what it means to teach students in a manner that prepares them for the world and on ways for the district to know whether or not it is working. She has ideas, of course; and in her mind she has defined what ultimate success will look like for the Ridgemont education system, even if the means of codifying measurement are yet to be discovered or defined. "How will I know when it's working?" she asks. "I'll know it's working when the kids who graduate from Ridgemont stand out as being better prepared for anything that comes at them than kids from any other school. I'll know it's working when a student that comes from a background of multigenerational poverty learns the skills and knowledge that help him change that paradigm. I'll know it's working the same way I know it's working now—when people go above and beyond to educate and support the kids in this school. When kids who leave this school come back and tell us how having been here made them better at whatever they end up doing. That's how I'll know."

In the meantime, Emmy has to settle for anecdote and observation. She has to uncover the small moments and insights that give her the confidence that everything is on the right track. There may come a time at which Ridgemont creates a better way of enabling and measuring student success, a way that fundamentally changes how education gets done not only here, but also elsewhere and everywhere.

Until then, Emmy and the Ridgemont schools can only focus on the task in front of them: working together to on Designing the Future, to think beyond standardized tests and focus on educating good people.

"People will tell us that what's happening in Ridgemont is amazing," she says. "But we always tell them, 'You haven't seen amazing yet.'"

Section II

THE SIX ATTRIBUTES OF IRRESISTIBLE SCHOOLS

14

REIMAGINING THE EDUCATIONAL EXPERIENCE

So how can the built environment play its role? Clearly, if students and their individual educational needs are so different, the physical spaces must move beyond the traditional classroom model. This is the question that SHP Leading Design puts to its clients, many of which express similar shifts in teaching and learning philosophies: human-centered, action-oriented, mindful of process, and observational and interactive.

This approach requires a curriculum that includes problem-solving activities, group work, team teaching and self-guided learning. The first and most obvious response is technology in the classroom. And why wouldn't it be? Today's students are very, very different than they were even five years ago. But technology is just part of the equation. SHP Leading Design believes that delivering education that changes the model for the better begins with the overarching educational vision.

For more than a century, SHP has been working collaboratively with educators, parents, school boards and students to create holistic learning environments. Sometimes that means envisioning a new school from the ground up. Other times it means reimagining existing facilities.

Either way, the goal is energetic spaces that encourage inter-disciplinary study and experimentation. And it starts by imagining, or reimagining, the educational experience from start to finish. SHP engages its clients in this planning and design process, with an eye toward ferreting out how school spaces can encourage different methods of teaching and styles of learning.

The SHP process also identifies challenges and opportunities that our clients face at the classroom, school and even district levels. What often arises from this educational visioning process are specific spaces—and sometimes entire buildings—that wrap around and support that curriculum, allowing students to learn in their own ways, at their own pace and in their own space.

Special care is given to enabling ownership of the learning environment by the students themselves. 21st-century learners need to have more room, literally, to take responsibility for their education.

No student can truly own his or her education in the rigid "cells and bells" classrooms that became commonplace nearly a century ago and still exist in many schools today. Instead, they need a learning environment that adapts day by day and minute by minute. One that supports a traditional classroom, small-group projects and self-directed learning. Space that enables flow from one activity to the next and throughout classrooms, corridor and outdoor learning environments.

The Ridgemont Local School District case study that you just read captures the essence of this approach.

When a full-scale renovation or new build isn't possible, incremental changes are a good option. Deer Park High School, near Cincinnati, is a perfect example of small changes that are possible. Like any typical high school kids, Deer Park students wanted "cool" spaces that didn't look like traditional classrooms. Educators wanted—and needed—classrooms that emulated a real-world environment, allowed for individual learning and group work, and still integrated digital devices.

The school used grant monies to expand its Career Academy

courses in areas like digital design, engineering, cyber security, health informatics and culinary arts. To support the expanded curriculum, SHP transformed the high school's lower level, to provide students with a real-world learning environment. That included team breakout rooms, mock-interview spaces and classrooms with seamless connectivity for all devices, as well as innovative spaces for group work, team teaching and traditional, large-group instruction. And then there was hands-on, experiential learning.

In the Beavercreek City School District, near Dayton, Ohio, a portion of the curriculum has been redesigned to focus on design thinking. To support this, SHP created four 2,000-square-foot design spaces, or d-labs, to help the district incorporate design and "maker space" collaboration for eighth- through 12th-grade students. Agile furniture with unique twists—imagine five-gallon paint buckets with padded, removable lids that kids use as both seats and storage—can be grouped and regrouped around mobile work tables, to encourage collaboration and support different lesson plans. A variety of surfaces, from high-tech smartboards to low-tech portable whiteboards, helps students bring their ideas to life.

Beyond obvious sustainable design characteristics, such as daylight harvesting, reduced energy use, sustainable materials, improved air quality and renewable energy sources, SHP designs schools that can evolve with students, technology and pedagogy. It is the ability to adapt to the changing needs of districts, schools and even individual spaces that defines a school as sustainable. School systems demand this flexibility. SHP delivers designs that can be easily renovated and reimagined as needs change. In today's fast-moving, ever changing world, one constant has emerged: It is incumbent upon every child to be a self-motivated, autonomous learner. Educators and parents know this, and changing educational philosophies and classroom teaching models reflect the shift.

Now it is time for the design community to enable the flexibility—in physical space and the built environment—that will encourage individualized learning.

15

WHAT IT WILL MEAN
TO LEARN IN THE FUTURE

Redefining our work as designers and architects and creating a new vision for educational space in America represent not just a major shift in SHP's business model, but a change in thinking about what it means to be a learner. Too often we think of education in the aggregate. We judge success in schools by the percentage of students who graduate. We fund districts based upon aggregate test scores. We judge a graduate looking for a job on the reputation of the school that they graduated from.

But education and learning are not macro-endeavors. Instead, learning is a lifelong pursuit by an individual. As we've worked to refine and polish our vision as a company, we have established a set of six attributes that we believe will serve as a basis for what it means to learn and facilitate learning for decades to come. These attributes serve both as a guide for our business and a measure of success in our thinking. They keep us focused on the work that we want to do and serve as design principles for the projects that we undertake.

In all cases these attributes put an emphasis on the individual, not the aggregate. We believe very deeply that a person learns, while people are educated. So many of the struggles and challenges that face our education system are rooted in the idea of working from the whole back to the individual. We believe making education better means beginning with the individual and solving for that person's needs. If we are able to do that consistently, it will improve the whole.

It's like writing a book. If we approached writing a book in the way that our national conversation and trends have approached education, we'd spend all of our time judging through standards of a concept. We'd change laws and create standards based on completed books. But ask any writer how they approach writing well, and they will tell you that they focus on one word or sentence at a time. The result of that kind of focus on picking the right word every time is a better book. It's the same with education. We, as a country, have spent a century looking at the results and making decisions based upon the aggregate. But now is the time to focus less on the forest and instead concentrate on producing healthy trees.

At SHP, we have defined six attributes, which embody and reflect our core belief of what education can and should be. These six attributes are focus areas for our company, but also the key attributes of education that defies current expectations, education that will empower the world in the future.

1. **Lifelong Learning** – education in the future will not be contained to early life.
2. **Whole-Life Learning** – future learning will break down the wall between our education lives (student lives) and the rest of our lives. We summarize points #1 and #2 with "L3 learning." This is learning that is life-long, life-wide and life-deep.
3. **Individualized Learning** – technology, accessibility and opportunity will mean a shift from learning en masse to learning tailored to a person's needs.
4. **Involved and Blended Learning** – the workforce and community will play a much more direct role in education.
5. **Unburdened Collaboration** – students, generations and teachers will benefit from each other's strengths.

6.   **Adaptive and Dynamic Space** – in the built environment and beyond for maximum flexibility in our everchanging world.

These six attributes serve as challenges for our firm, ideals that we plan to explore and expand upon, to innovate against and toward. After more than a century of designing schools, we now face the challenge of reimagining education.

16

ATTRIBUTE #1: LIFELONG LEARNING

We need to shift our thinking from education as a one-time-of-life event to an ongoing process that follows a person throughout their entire life. The idea of "getting an education" is a flawed way of looking at things.

As we look 10 years into the future, we know that we will have over five generations in the workforce. Global labor shortages and the extension of the professional lives of senior citizens will make us reconsider the education, and re-education, of these people.

"Education and training will become more important," writer, speaker and scenario thinker Richard Watson puts it plainly in his book *The Future Files: the 5 trends that will shape the next 50 years*. "In the case of adults, this means lifelong learning. The idea here is that the education needs to be a continuous process due to the rapid change brought about by science, technology and globalization. However, for most people, if they think they need it, it will already be too late."

We need to see each person as a lifelong learner. Creating multiple generations of learners will have a strong and needed effect on how we interact with technology.

Nicholas Carr is a technology, business and culture writer. He originally came to prominence with the 2003 *Harvard Business Review* article "IT Doesn't Matter." In it and a number of other works, he argues that the strategic importance of information technology in business has diminished as IT has become more commonplace, standardized and cheaper.

In 2014, Carr published *The Glass Cage: Automation and Us.* It provides a critical examination of the role of computer automation in contemporary life, from historical, technical, economic and philosophical viewpoints. In both works, Carr cautions that technology alone will not solve our problems: It will *become* the problem, if left unchecked. "As computer systems and software applications come to play an ever larger role in shaping our lives and the world, we have an obligation to be more, not less, involved in decisions about their design and use—before technological momentum forecloses our options. We should be careful about what we make."

If we have multiple generations working and learning together, how do we ensure that the learning of the previous generation is absorbed by the generation that follows? All too often we skip over previous lessons learned and repeat the same mistakes.

"In our pioneer and agrarian beginnings, we were close to the land, and the laws of nature were evident," Gary Johnson, SHP's senior field representative, says. "We learned, say, about the species of trees that were good for one or more uses, while others were not. What wood is naturally rot-resistant? Which is fine for furniture, but bad if used in contact with the earth? Why are baseball bats made from only a few specific tree species? Why is white oak good for whiskey barrels, but red oak is absolutely not?

"We may Google the properties that we desire and find a fine fit for the listed properties, only to find that in practical use it may be impossible. If you don't know the difference, this is a chance to learn from a source that has already solved these issues and may not be readily available in our normal course of study.

"There is an opportunity to teach youngsters and even an older generation—a course of study that may only be taught by a generation ahead of them to reap information that has already been established and possibly forgotten by most. By the same token, we cannot wait for all of the oldies to die off to have everyone computer or technology literate. Obviously technology advances daily, and we will never be caught up. Young people with patience could help educate those of a previous generation, a skill developed after their so-called 'learning years' have come and gone."

What does this mean for education and lifelong learners? It means that the knowledge of five generations in the workforce is needed. Technology alone is just a tool. We need to think differently about what makes us smart. "What really makes us smart," Carr writes, "is not our ability to pull facts from documents or decipher statistical patterns in arrays of data. It's our ability to make sense of things, to weave the knowledge we draw from observations and experience, from *living*, into a rich and fluid understanding of the world that we can then apply to any task or challenge. It's this supple quality of mind, spanning conscious and unconscious, reason and inspiration, that allows human beings to think conceptually, critically, metaphorically, speculatively—to take leaps of logic and imagination."

Technology, science and culture will continue to change. As Carr points out, we need to focus on what we are asking the technology to do and what differentiates human intelligence from machine intelligence. Lifelong learners are not just a reality for the future of education; they will be important for how future generations imagine, design and build that future.

The Baby Boomers sit at one end of the lifelong-learners spectrum; and at the other end, we find Generation Z, a group of people who have never known a time without the Internet, social networks, smartphones and apps. Yet, in the midst of this amazing technology, the only America they've known has been in a constant state of war, with the whole world sinking into a global recession. This generation knows that they will likely not make more money than their parents' generation. This gives them a vastly different view of the meaning and value of education.

They are not alone. The Millennials—the generation just before Generation Z—are the first generation that will in all likelihood retire with student-loan debt. The global recession has taken away over a decade of earnings and savings from them. Their long-term financial stability and retirement are far more tenuous than that of previous generations.

Both the Millennials and Generation Z are producing a cultural change and paradigm shift. Will these generations continue their education in the traditional way? Will they want to send their own children to a traditional university, when they are still paying off their own college debt? These factors might reshape what future generations expect for their own lifelong learning and for the education of their children, as well.

17

ATTRIBUTE #2:
WHOLE-LIFE LEARNING

In order for lifelong learning to truly take hold, we must consider the whole life of the learner, including their family and community. We predict an expanded role for life coaches and mentors in our models of future education methods. This path includes not only traditional job training (acquiring specific skills), but also becoming a well-rounded human being and citizen of the world.

With this "whole-life" style of education, we will still focus on the fundamentals (reading, writing, science and math), but will also become more expansive, helping students with specific jobs, internships and personal growth. Businesses need to interact early with the learner, setting them up for multiple careers, while also balancing the development of both knowledge and skills by placing a premium on each learner's IQ (intelligence quotient) *and* EQ (emotional quotient).

In many ways education will be less about the school and more about the whole life of the learner. Research shows that the school itself can have a smaller impact on the life of the learner than we would like to think.

In their bestselling book *Freakonomics: A Rogue Economist Explores the Hidden Side of Everything,* University of Chicago economist Steven Levitt and *New York Times* journalist Stephen J. Dubner took an unconventional approach to big problems. They examined not only schools, but also the biggest factor in the lives of younger learners: parents. "...just about every parent seems to believe that her child will thrive if only he can attend the *right* school," they wrote. "The [school] with an appropriate blend of academics, extracurricular, friendliness and safety."

To test this the authors dug into data about schools. "In 1980 the U.S. Department of Justice and the Chicago Board of Education teamed up to try and better integrate the city's schools. It was decreed that incoming freshmen could apply to virtually any high school in the district....So what did the data reveal? In this case, the school choice barely mattered at all."

Levitt and Dubner uncovered that the academic success of the learners in the studies had little to do with the actual school that they attended. It had more to do with their parents and their communities. "Could it really be that school choice doesn't much matter?" they asked. "No self-respecting parent, obsessive or otherwise, is ready to believe that."

To get a better picture, Levitt and Dubner looked at a larger study of American schools. "In the late 1990s, the U.S. Department of Education undertook a monumental project called Early Childhood Longitudinal Study," they explained. "The ECLS sought to measure the academic progress of more than twenty thousand children from kindergarten through fifth grade. The subjects were chosen from across the country to represent an accurate cross section of American school children."

The findings were even more shocking than in Chicago. Levitt and Dubner learned that academic success had little to do with the physical school that the child attended and even less to do with what parents actively did. "Parents who are well educated, successful, and healthy tend to have children who test well in school but it doesn't much matter whether a child is trotted off to museums or spanked or sent to Head Start....If you are smart, hardworking, well educated, well paid and married to someone equally fortunate then your children are more likely to succeed.

"But it isn't so much a matter of what you do as a parent; it's who you are. In this regard, an overbearing parent is a lot like a political candidate who believes that money wins elections—whereas in truth, all the money in the world can't get a candidate elected if the voters don't like him to start with."

Levitt and Dubner's study illuminates an uncomfortable fact: Schools alone may not make well-rounded learners. The learner's family, community and environment have more to do with success. We believe the future will mean seeing schools and education as something that moves throughout the life of the learner, involving everyone from that person's life. An emphasis on the learner's community can be just as important as focusing on the physical school and what goes on within its walls.

Limiting education to schools might be tradition, but it's limiting. We must ask ourselves what would happen if education became a fundamental reality in a systemic way. Many people are already approaching learning as a lifelong activity. But if lifelong learning became the norm, and that learning was based on holistic approaches that involved family and community—that stretched and spread well beyond the walls of schools—what impact might that have on public discourse? How would we think about generations teaching each other? How might a more fluid and dynamic approach to education serve to redefine our society as a whole?

These are lofty questions, to be sure, but essential ones. The more inclusive we can begin to make education now and in the context of physical structures, the greater the expectations we create for the future, and the wider the impact might be felt. It begins by bringing the outside world into the schools and taking what's happening in the schools out to the larger world.

At SHP we have, for many years, sought outside input into the design of schools, in order to meet community needs. But that is only one step. In order to make education a fully inclusive experience and an essential part of life, we need to develop the same rigor in seeking input into the design of education itself.

18

ATTRIBUTE #3:
INDIVIDUALIZED LEARNING

We can turn nearly anything into a computer, and we are surrounded by computational intelligence. Technology has transformed nearly every aspect of our lives—the way we shop, communicate and share, even the way we get around in the physical world. Every interaction with technology produces data that is then used to create predictive modeling for what we might do next.

If you book an airline ticket online, hotels in the area of your destination will be recommended. If you read an article and share it on Facebook, you'll soon see similar topics showing up in your feed. If you make a purchase on Amazon, the site will recommend related items to you when you return.

So much of our modern culture is shaped by the notion of mass personalization. Why should education be any different? Why do we insist that it is? Every time you see a headline about education, it is written from the perspective of the mass—graduation rates, pass rates, the rates in which students are going to college, the cumulative student debt.

But isn't education, perhaps more than any other endeavor, a personal one? Of course! In a world of mass personalization through technology, shouldn't we be able to approach education from a near-microscopic perspective of the individual needs of the student? If Amazon can understand your preference in backpacks and predict your needs, why can't education understand your interests and aptitudes and predict your course direction and learning needs?

John Naisbitt is a legend in the world of futures and long-term strategic thinking. His 1982 book *Megatrends: Ten Directions Transforming our Lives* was wildly popular. It explored the late-20th-century shift from an industrial society to an information age. He introduced business audiences around the world to the coming futures. Even in 1982, he recognized that computers would make education more individual. "First, computers offer a cost-effective albeit capital intensive way of individualizing education," he wrote. "Second, computers simplify the extensive record keeping required for individualized instruction. Third, familiarity with computers is now considered a strong vocational advantage, a salable skill."

Naisbitt's prescient vision of individualized education has exploded in the 21st-century. By harnessing the power of big data, as well as personalized learning, we can understand and know the respective learner, producing a genuinely individualized learning experience. This includes not only the basic educational needs of the learner, but also the goals and aspirations of the learner throughout their entire life.

But technology will not solve everything. As we move toward a future of individualized learning, we must resist the temptation to think of technology as a panacea for education.

Salman Kahn's Kahn Lab School in Silicon Valley explores how current technologies might individualize education. Kahn, the creator of the online education giant Kahn Academy, is testing out new approaches and was featured in a November 2015 *Wired Magazine* profile. "His team is diligently recording and tracking every student's progress and sharing that finding with their parents and staff, an open source approach to educational innovation," writer Jason Tanz reported. "Every week, students set their own academic goals—the level of math they hope to master, the amount of time they plan to dedicate to reading and so on....Unlike many progressive schools, the Lab School is a firm believer in standardized testing—students are evaluated three times a year, the better to measure their progress and make sure the school is living up to expectations. 'It's not acceptable for even one student in this school to not grow as expected,' Kahn says, 'and hopefully all of them are growing two to three times as expected.'

"One of the tenets of the Lab School is that kids should play an active role in designing their own education," Tanz adds. "This means that a lot of the school day is spent discussing the school itself."

Individualized learning is being realized in small pockets across the country and the world, thanks to our modern technology. By keeping a pragmatic eye on what we want that technology to achieve and not falling for the tech hype, we move ever closer to a future of individualized learning.

The individualization of education, mixed with the idea of life-long learners, could also give rise to some interesting shifts in the culture and decision-making process for how people determine where they get their education. This includes where people choose to pursue their education throughout their lives, as well as where parents choose to start their children in the lifelong learning process.

"People will always measure the value of skills and personal advancement in regard to how they affect social relationships," says Steve Tossey, a senior mechanical engineer at SHP. "They will ask, 'Will this improve my marriage and/or friendships? Will this make me a better citizen? Will it better qualify me for this job I want?' But in addition, employers and other leaders will want a person to have some recognizable credentials, before hiring or auditioning."

Where we get our education will shift over time, depending upon the needs of the person. Schools will, in short, become personalized approaches to education and not merely brick-and-mortar facilities. This is not to say that the experience of going to school— particularly for young people—is not valuable. Quite the contrary, in fact. The socialization that occurs in a built environment will continue to be vitally important. And we continue to have personal reasons for selecting a school—family legacy, program offerings, specific job training, etc...—but education will no longer be bound to the physical facility.

Technology will not "solve" education; but our ability to create, disseminate and access learning will open a world of possibilities, in terms of how we learn and, hopefully, how we talk about education— as an individual pursuit, not simply a topic of the day.

19

ATTRIBUTE #4:
INVOLVED AND BLENDED LEARNING

The forces of technology, culture and economics are placing a massive amount of pressure on existing educational systems. Universities provide an interesting case study for this shift, as illustrated by "Creative Destruction," a profile in *The Economist* from June 2014.

"Now a revolution has begun, thanks to three forces; rising costs, changing demand and disruptive technologies. The result will be the reinvention of the university," according to the piece. "Whereas the price of cars, computers and much else have fallen dramatically, universities, protected by public-sector funding and the premium employers place on degrees, have been able to charge ever more for the same service."

The article continues by pointing out that the cost of college has outpaced inflation for more than two decades. This rising debt is carried not only by college graduates, but also by those who do not graduate (which, in the U.S., is more than 40 percent of students who attend college). The economics of higher education are reason enough to re-examine the model; but couple them with how technology is changing the nature and availability of work for graduates, and the need becomes crystal clear.

Automation is beginning to have the same effect on white-collar jobs as it has on blue-collar ones. According to a study from Oxford University, 47 percent of occupations are at risk of being automated in the next few decades. As innovation reduces or eliminates some jobs and changes others, people will need to adapt throughout their lives.

Even by themselves, cost and changing demand would be pushing change. But rapidly changing technology ensures it. The Internet, which has turned many business models upside down (retail, books, the music industry, etc.), will upend higher education.

A blended model is not only important for the future of learners; it is also desperately needed for the economic well-being of the educational system.

Who funds and interacts with these schools changes, as well. New approaches for education need to be built on models that flex and change, depending upon the needs of the learner. Often it might be traditional skills and test-based learning in early development, but eventually the involvement of industry and specific companies will expand. Funding and participation could come from public/private/ nonprofit/self-funded or military sources.

Schools become involved in people's lives and communities in radically different ways. No longer are they single-use physical spaces, but a blend of traditional and nontraditional sources (e.g., charter schools, home schools), when appropriate. The use of the built environment becomes more fluid, blending not just with learner's needs, but with the community and local/global industry.

This blending and flexibility of purpose give education and schools an increased role in the lives of learners. It is this flexibility of the business model, paired with an understanding of the needs of each community, that will feed the health of the educational system.

Computer scientist Jaron Lanier is no stranger to technology; but in his 2010 book *You are not a Gadget,* he cautions that "Facebook is similar to No Child Left Behind. Information systems need to have information in order to run, but information underrepresents reality. Demand more from information than it can give, and you end up with monstrous designs. Under the No Child Left Behind Act of 2002, for example, U.S. teachers were often forced to choose between teaching general knowledge and 'teaching to the test.' The best teachers are thus often disenfranchised by the improper use of educational information systems.

"What computerized analysis of all of the country's school tests has done to education is exactly what Facebook has done to friendships," Lanier points out. "In both cases, life is turned into a database. Both degradations are based on the same philosophical mistake, which is the belief that computers can presently represent human thought or relationships. These are things computers cannot currently do."

The involvement of the community and local businesses is needed to offset, to humanize the increased use of technology for education. Although technology can provide many benefits, it is the blended model that will help balance the schools and better serve the learners.

20

ATTRIBUTE #5:
UNBURDENED COLLABORATION

We believe a school will not always be physical; thus traditional ideas of distance and separation fall away. We will see unburdened collaboration between people and schools, and even among individual learners. Schools can be wherever we need them to be. New spaces that have never been schools can become schools on demand.

Similarly, the locations of the individual learners become less important. Their proximity to physical schools matters less and less, but what matters even less is their proximity to other learners and the educational system that they need.

The idea that people would no longer have to worry about the distances that separate them is not new. It was discussed back in the 20th century by journalist Frances Cairncross of *The Economist*, in his book *The Death of Distance*. Based on evidence from two sweeping surveys on telecommunications, he argued that new communications technologies were rapidly obliterating distance as a relevant factor in how we conduct our business and personal lives.

But in November 2013, journalist Phillip Longman pushed back on Cairncross's vision in "The Myth of Technology and the Death of Distance," published on Politico. "They promised us a world where geography wouldn't matter," Longman begins. "As everything in our lives moved online, the best and brightest would scatter to the hinter-lands, leaving only decaying urban wastelands in their wake. One of the most enthusiastic technophiles of the early Internet age, George Gilder, proclaimed in 1995 that cities were just 'leftover baggage from the industrial era' and that 'all of the monopolies and hierarchies and pyramids and power grids of industrial society are going to dissolve.' Not to be outdone, *The Economist* announced in 1995 that the communications revolution would bring nothing less than 'the death of distance.'"

We know, of course, that this vision did not become reality. Contrary to the predictions, technology and the digital age brought about a mass influx to cities in the U.S. and around the world, rather than the exodus that seemed predestined.

This digital urbanization reveals a truth about technology: While we may be able to telecommute to work, in order to innovate and learn, we need other people. Communications technologies have greatly collapsed distance and time for many people. The ways in which we learn and work have morphed and changed, as we've moved into the 21st century. Technology might bring about a new kind of unburdened collaboration for people and education, but we must remember that there are vast cultural and economic divides that have not been addressed.

Unburdened collaboration in learning will mean integrating technology, as well as exploring new ways for learners to work with teachers, mentors, other learners and influencers who will be crucial to their education. By encouraging collaboration over curriculum, we encourage conversations and exchange; and technology becomes a medium for crossing divides, not a solution to them.

21

ATTRIBUTE #6:
ADAPTIVE AND DYNAMIC SPACES

Advances in digital technologies and material science mean that schools can become both digitally adaptive and physically dynamic. In fact, the digital and the physical must work together.

"Whenever people imagine virtual anything, they immediately pit it against its physical counterpart," wrote Salman Kahn in his *Scientific American* thought piece "No More Lockstep Learning: Technology can humanize the classroom." He continued, "Amazon versus physical book store, Wikipedia versus physical encyclopedias. They assume that the virtual will replace the physical with something cheaper, faster and more efficient. In education, however, the virtual will create a very different type of disruption. We should not aim to replace the physical classroom. Instead we have an opportunity to blend the virtual with the physical and reimagine education entirely."

The interplay between the physical and the virtual opens up a wide range of opportunities for education. With the increased use of virtual and augmented reality, what can the built and designed world teach the digital? When materials become smart and can change their forms, how will they interact with learners? How will they interact with the data itself?

We don't need to look far to see how technology and physical structures can work together. From the increasingly ubiquitous smartboard- and Wi-Fi-enabled classrooms to students Facetiming with astronauts on the International Space Station, technology needs to be seen as an adaptable, nimble tool to help improve the quality of education. And the possibilities that we see in the technological world should be inspiration for the built one.

At SHP, we've been reimagining schools to be more than just "cells and bells." In a collaborative, inclusive, individualized educational world, the school building can be either an empowering tool or an impediment. And we've seen lately just how powerful a built environment can be in helping to solidify a different model for learning. When spaces are built in service of a larger vision, when they are designed to adapt, to move, to fluctuate and bend in service of students' needs, they hardly ever end up looking like the schools of the 20th century.

The Ridgemont School District project in particular embodies the starting point of possibility for redesigning education. Of the thousands that SHP has worked on over more than a century, this is the one that provides a glimpse into the future and demonstrates the power of what can happen when educators, industry, students and a community come together to create a new vision for learning.

A few years ago, the tiny school district in central Ohio was just like any other small district in the country. The schools were traditionally designed and showing their age. Teachers were expected to teach toward standardized tests. The community had grown apathetic toward what was happening in the schools, which were essentially warehouses for students, places for them to learn the three R's and move on.

But an amazing transformation happened—not just because of our work, but because of the decisions that the community made to create a better approach to education. This is why the Ridgemont example deserves a deeper look.

As SHP works diligently to help redefine education from mass to individual; from contained to lifelong; from isolated to including the whole lives of learners; from walled off to involved and blended; from rote to collaborative; and from rigid to adaptive, Ridgemont gives us a blueprint on which to build.

CONCLUSION
9 BILLION SCHOOLS

The Ridgemont project in many ways embodied the six attributes that we believe will be necessary building blocks of individualized lifelong learning.

The agriculture program embodied the spirit of lifelong learning by giving students real-world experiences and a framework for continued learning after graduation.

Community involvement in the Envisioning Day and beyond demonstrated how considering a student's whole life—their family, their mentors, their future employers—can impact not only what they learn, but how.

The importance placed on project- and service-based learning gave students the freedom and responsibility for pursuing individualized learning. It also encouraged—and even mandated—unburdened collaboration among students, their teachers and the community.

Team teaching, blended subjects and combining the needs of the students with the real-world challenges that they will face after graduation demonstrated the involved and blended learning that we see as paramount for education's evolution.

And the building itself—with movable furniture, sliding walls, collaboration spaces, student meeting rooms, common areas and other features not often seen in a school district the size of Ridgemont—demonstrated how technology and the built environment can work together, to create adaptive and dynamic contexts for learning.

But as proud as we are of the work that we did on Ridgemont, we know the project is merely a harbinger of things to come—the tip of the educational iceberg.

Our vision for individualized lifelong learning will be fully realized when we can take the lessons learned from Ridgemont and expand further and deeper into the lives of learners. We've developed a model that we hope will guide our firm into the future—a future we help to design that will be built upon the six key attributes laid out in this book.

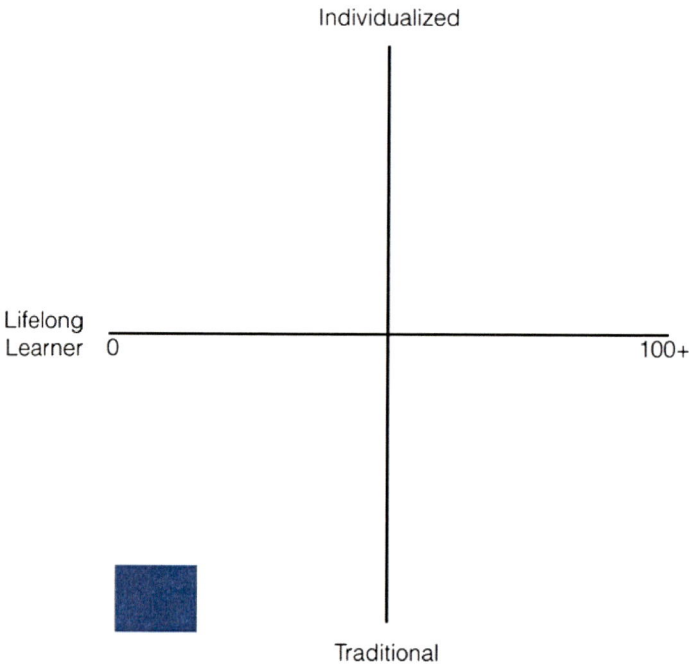

Individualized

Lifelong
Learner   0   100+

Traditional

On the horizontal axis is the life of the learner, from birth to 100 years old and beyond. The vertical axis represents progress from traditional "cells and bells" education, in which students are taught standard lessons en masse, to fully realized individual education.

For most of SHP's history, indeed since the first days of standardized industrial education, learning and schools were relegated to the lower left quadrant of this model.

Education was limited to early life. Even after higher education went from being the exception to the rule, formal learning was restricted to early life. Being a learner meant being a student, and being a student represented a specific time in life before people were expected to join the workforce and build a career.

The Ridgemont project, with its emphasis on service and project-based learning, the integration of community and industry into the curriculum and, indeed, the school itself, was a step in the right direction. Students are and will be encouraged to make education an ongoing ambition, something to pursue even after graduation. With Emmy Beeson's vision and our flexible, adaptable design, learning is also more collaborative and individualized at the same time.

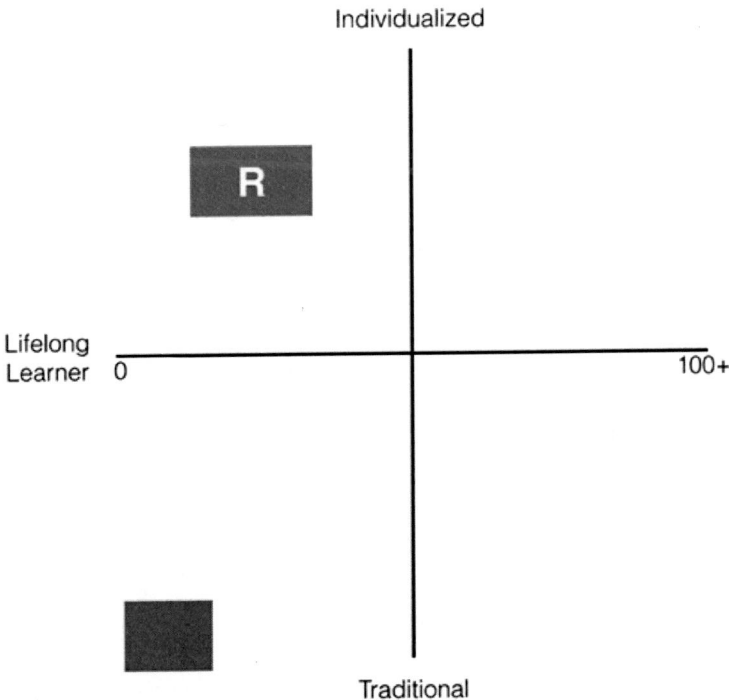

Individualized

R

Lifelong
Learner   0   100+

Traditional

The advances that we have made with the Ridgemont project move our vision closer to reality, but the influence of formalized education is still limited to early life. And, as individual as student projects are, success—and funding—will still be based upon the achievement of the larger student body.

When developing our vision as a company—as architects, designers, technologists and educational futurists—we set our sights higher. We know the path to the future will be laid with iterative improvements and guided by the six attributes: Lifelong, Whole Life, Individualized, Involved and Blended Unburdened Collaboration, Adaptive and Dynamic. It will require advancements in technology and materials, changes in policies that dictate school funding and initiatives. We will need to rethink educational models, teacher training and expectations in the workforce. We will be forced to tackle the challenges that have perplexed many into a state of stasis, the apathy and distance that have created contempt for some and disheartened others. We will need to develop the discipline to constantly challenge ourselves, to challenge the status quo and to demand better for students and ourselves.

But as the old saying goes, the best time to plant a tree is 50 years ago, and the second best time is now. Without taking action and forcing ourselves to think about what education can and should be now, we will never change the future. And it seems like everywhere you look in society, the future is defined by change. This is not a pie-in-the-sky, wouldn't-it-be-nice scenario. We are not, as SHP, calling for a revolution in learning, but merely joining one. Technology, connected culture and common sense are allowing us to challenge the way that we expect to learn. Changes in the workforce not only allow us to continue our education well beyond our student years, but also make continued learning imperative. Rising tuition costs and mounting student debt, along with changing career expectations and opportunities, are giving many pause and others incentive to innovate, within and without the system.

Education needs an overhaul now, much in the same way

that it did a century and a half ago, when schools began to take the place of fireside lessons. We need to change the perception of what it means to be a learner, as much as we change the practice of learning.

But it won't happen just because an architecture and design firm believes it should. It will only happen when everyone comes to see himself or herself as a stakeholder, when communities and generations, educators and industries come together to formulate and commit to a new vision for how we learn.

That is the real lesson of Ridgemont.

Education is more than just the imparting of information. Schools are more than just holding pens for students. But defining what "more" means requires thought beyond standardization, vision beyond need. The leaders of Ridgeway and Mount Victory, Ohio, came together to define "more" for their students; and doing so required a reexamination of what they wanted for their community.

If we are to reshape our education for the students of tomorrow, we must reexamine the kind of world in which we want to live and act accordingly. We must think not only of their success, but also of our own.

To help create a framework for the kind of bold thinking—and acting—that we need for a true 21st century, SHP Leading Design is helping to foster a movement called 9 Billion Schools. In 2050, there will be more than nine billion people on the planet, and we believe that there should be nine billion schools. Not literal structures, of course, but a way of thinking that every single person is, in essence, a school unto him- or herself, a "place" of continual learning from birth to death. We hope you will join us in helping to realize this vision. Learn more at www.9billionschools.org.

Made in the USA
San Bernardino, CA
22 November 2017